# A HISTORY
# OF THE NEWBERY
# AND CALDECOTT
# MEDALS

# A HISTORY

*of the*

# NEWBERY

*and*

# CALDECOTT MEDALS

*by*

## IRENE SMITH

NEW YORK · THE VIKING PRESS

*Dedicated to*

*Clara  Whitehill  Hunt*

*and  to*

*the  past  and  present  children's  librarians*

*in  the  Brooklyn  Public  Library;*

*also  to*

*those  intrepid  readers,*

*the  children  of  Brooklyn*

# ACKNOWLEDGMENTS

If I were to list all the persons who have helped me with their recollections and information, I am afraid that this small volume might seem to make pretentious claims, to the discredit of their generosity. Readers, too, could be misled in their expectations of the contents, by a roster of its distinguished contributors. May I therefore simply thank all my friends and associates, active and retired, who have advised me, and whom I have quoted, with or without permission?

The letter files were treated as public domain. I thank their writers, in legion. The letters that Frederic G. Melcher wrote in thirty-five years on Medal affairs were the basic source of knowledge for this narrative. I hope this book reflects the influence of their enthusiasm and philosophy, as a best expression of the thanks I owe the Medals' donor.

IRENE SMITH

# Contents

# A HISTORY
# OF THE NEWBERY
# AND CALDECOTT
# MEDALS

# CHAPTER I

# *Three Bookmen True*

An event long established in the American calendar of children's books and libraries has linked in common cause, across all barriers of time, an eighteenth-century London publisher, a nineteenth-century English illustrator, and a twentieth-century New York editor. The substance of this event is two yearly prizes in children's literature, named in honor of John Newbery, who published children's books two centuries ago, and Randolph Caldecott, a picture-book artist one century after Newbery. These latter-day honors endow the two elder bookmen with contemporary fame far outdistancing that which could have been imaginable to them in their own times. Their renewed tradition, engraved upon two bronze medals, is the inspiration and the gift of an editor-publisher in our time, Frederic Gershom Melcher. In the annals of children's literature these Medals that stand for achievement bind together three gentlemen well destined for kinship—Newbery, Caldecott, and Melcher, bookmen of renown.

The Newbery and Caldecott Medals are given through the American Library Association by a member committee of children's and school librarians. Both Medals are awarded annually, the first for a contribution to children's literature, the latter for distinction in a picture book. Four exciting decades in the making of children's books have passed since the Newbery award was established in 1921. American literature for children began its ascent up the ladder of recognition, as an art and an influence, shortly after the First World War. The forces behind that sudden growth and expansion have been variously interpreted, as befits the many-sided attractions of a remarkably lively subject. Among all explanations of those forces of change, the Medals' story offers one distinct and ample theme, satisfying to record because of its dignity and idealism.

The story begins naturally with Frederic Melcher, who, until his death in 1963, kept its lifeblood flowing. He had brought the award plan into being at an American Library Association conference in Swampscott, Massachusetts, in June 1921. Melcher, at that time in his third year as an editor of *Publishers' Weekly,* was already a seasoned spokesman for the book business. If children's books held a close place with him, it was one kept warm with memories of boyhood reading in his New England home. The son of Edwin Forrest and Alice Bartlett Melcher was born in Malden, Massachusetts, six miles north of Boston, April 12, 1879. When Frederic was four they moved to Newton Center, another Boston suburb, whose salient advantage was a big pond. Here there was fishing in summer, ice-skating in winter, and fun to be had with boys of to be read. Melcher had discovered their insistent appeal. He recalled some early favorites for a volume published in his honor in 1945: *Frederic G. Melcher, Friendly*

*Century among Books and* d by the Book Publishers'

almost anything that came to ton] library was a place I fre- facilities were not what a town nineties there was no special t in this branch, and we took  large room there was a long for newspapers. I always read eekly, *Leslie's,* the *Illustrated American.* I had had *Youth's* by selling subscriptions, and *People* and *St. Nicholas.* There cept some few reference books r card the numbers which you atalogue or from the monthly arian did not expect to make  selections from authors we ad recommended. The author  get overlooked, but we read ers. Henty, G. A.; Castlemon, , Edward S.; Otis, James, see J. T.; Stephens, C. A.; Alger, Munroe, Kirk; these come

as from my own books and . Our home library was not Christmas and birthdays. The

---

Erratum

A HISTORY OF THE NEWBERY AND CALDECOTT MEDALS

Third printing

*The following lines were inadvertently dropped from bottom page 12.*

Frederic's own age the year around. There was also some growing up to be done, the public school and dancing school to attend, and all the while books, and more books,

books you owned you were likely to read several times. There was a brown stuffed chair between the bay window and the fireplace over the arm of which I could comfortably fling a leg and then nestle back for hours. Our one bookcase was just around the corner in the hall with a set of *Johnson's Encyclopedia* on the bottom shelf, an atlas, *Phil Sheridan's Memoirs, Innocents Abroad* in black cloth and *The Fireside Book of Poetry*. Other tall books were on the next shelf, including *Zigzag Journeys* to India and to the Antipodes, a couple of the Vassar Girl series which Sister owned, a *Last Days of Pompeii*, King's *Handbook of Boston, Recollections of the Auton House,* and a couple of *Brownie* books and other titles. The two upper shelves had our story books, *Little Men, An Old-Fashioned Girl, Neighbor Jackwood, Cudjo's Cave, The Cat of Bubastes, Huck Finn, Arabian Nights,* the various fairy tale books, *Little Lord Fauntleroy, Hans Brinker,* the *Dotty Dimple* series, a few volumes of Optic and Kellogg, the Jack Hazard Series, *The Young Moose Hunters, Winning His Way, Boys of '76, Jack Hall, Tom Brown at Rugby,* Longfellow's *Poems,* and Whittier's in double-columned octavos. I had three boy cousins in town of my own age and they and I and various school chums swapped books around.

Fred Melcher took the Institute Course at Newton High School, preparing for the Massachusetts Institute of Technology, but by the time of his graduation in 1895 he did not want to be a chemist or an engineer. As he had not taken enough Latin or Greek for entrance requirements in a liberal arts college, he quit school, and at sixteen quite accidentally got into the book business. He went to work dusting books for four dollars a week, in the long-famous Boston bookstore of Estes and Lauriat on Washington Street, opposite Old South Church.

"We get the picture of a slight, tallish youth dressed in a black alpaca working coat, alert, inclined to seriousness and not unduly given to skylarking with other boys in the basement mailing room," wrote Charles E. Goodspeed in *Friendly Reminiscences*—a book frequently quoted here.

Young Melcher began his life under experienced bookmen. After advancing from mail-opener and case-unpacker to clerk filling library orders, he learned to arrange stock and to appraise new books. Libraries found his judgment sound. His popularity with store customers grew. Eighteen years of selling books at Lauriat's passed, bringing him in 1912 to presidency of the Boston Booksellers' League.

Frederic Melcher had married Marguerite Fellows in 1910. They, with their son Daniel, moved in March 1913 to Indianapolis, where for the next five years Melcher was in charge of W. K. Stewart's bookstore. Stewart's in those days was a rendezvous of Vachel Lindsay, Albert Beveridge, George Ade, Booth Tarkington, James Whitcomb Riley, Meredith Nicholson, and Hoosiers of kindred spirit.

The Melchers moved back East when Mr. R. R. Bowker hired the young bookseller as co-editor of *Publishers' Weekly,* beginning May 1, 1918. The family, enlarged by a daughter, Nancy, born in Indianapolis, moved to Montclair, New Jersey. Within a few years they bought the old farmhouse at the edge of town, and this remained their home. Their third child, Charity, was born in Montclair.

Frederic Melcher, who soon established a growing liaison between publishers, booksellers, and librarians, had found his right place in the office of *Publishers'*

*Weekly*. His special gift was to make each group help the others, thereby helping all to help themselves. These groups must in any case have appreciated him for his warm human qualities, but, besides, they came to rely upon his concrete knowledge of their three-way problems.

That first year in New York it fell to Frederic Melcher, as Secretary of the American Booksellers Association, to organize a nationwide observance of Children's Book Week. Franklin K. Mathiews of the Boy Scouts of America had laid the foundation of a plan before World War I. Here was a definite channel for Melcher's interest in children's books, which had been rekindled by selling Howard Pyles and Louisa May Alcotts while he worked for Lauriat. Other channels developed; he recognized their possibilities and took action. He promptly commended Macmillan and, later, Doubleday, Page for appointing special editors of children's books. They were the first publishers to do so. In another channel Melcher began in 1920, abetted by co-editor Mildred Smith, to devote special issues of *Publishers' Weekly* to children's books. Three of these now appear each year, stimulating children's book departments in stores all over the country. The award medals that followed were consistent with Frederic Melcher's imaginative support of children's books, a support that was also practical and telling. The medals were to bring a fresh challenge to writers, to publishers, to dealers, and assuredly to librarians.

In Boston young Fred Melcher had come under the influence of D. Berkeley Updike, the famous printer. From him Melcher caught enthusiasm for beautiful books and the craftsmanship of bookmaking. Here too his influence was to be strongly felt through many years that followed. "If it's a well-made book it *feels* right and you feel right about it," he said. A past president of the American Institute of Graphic Arts, Melcher was cited by that body in 1945, "In recognition of his many-sided contributions to the Graphic Arts through fifty years; his patient and judicial sponsorship of worthy causes, international as well as national; his continuing kindly encouragement of young men and women first entering the world of books; and his tireless, accomplished, and successful efforts to make known and to maintain high standards of bookmaking." Not surprisingly, Melcher was one of those who established the Graphic Arts annual selection, "Fifty Books of the Year."

Much more could be told: of his rise to presidency of the R. R. Bowker Company, publishers to the American book trade; of the international book meetings and congresses of publishers at which he represented the United States; of his citations, civic activities, and hobbies—among which the collection of books on the history and practices of the book trade is supreme. His fellow citizen of Montclair, Margery Quigley, wrote for *Library Journal* when it surprised him with a special tribute, "Fred is a happy, generous person, completely without cynicism. In ethics and politics he is watchful, fearless, and liberal. He has a grand time with his family, even to his distant kin and their children's children, with his friends in their homes and in his, and with thousands of chance acquaintances. . . ."

In 1945 Frederic G. Melcher completed fifty years in his profession. The occasion was marked with an extraordinary succession of honors and expressions of affection. The most gala of these occurred on a May evening when seven hundred publishers, booksellers, and librarians gathered in the Waldorf-Astoria ballroom for a testimonial dinner. The happy year was marked by children's librarians of the American Library Association with a gift to their friend: two books from the old firm of John Newbery, *Tom Telescope,* published in 1761, and *Pretty Poems for Children Six Feet High,* published in 1757; and a set of picture books by Randolph Caldecott in the original printing, all sixteen of them in a red case.

A few distinguished friends, themselves book people, assembled a collection of papers about Melcher for the *Friendly Reminiscences* volume, which marked his first half-century of work at the book trade. In it Christopher Morley wrote:

Zeal is an old-fashioned word, but I can't think of anyone more zealous than Frederic Melcher. The number of books, schemes, ideas, transactions, ceremonies, speeches, promotions, dinners, awards, conferences, editorials, articles that have passed through his mind, leaving, apparently, no trace of erosion or corrugations on his brow, staggers me to contemplate.

This twentieth-century bookman was gifted with a diversity of talents. His companions in our Medal triumvirate were specialists, but the widest stretches of the field have felt his reach. "His absolute freedom from self-seeking is one of the secrets of his amazing accomplishment," wrote Bertha Mahony Miller. "His approaches to books and to people have always been infused with life and enthusiasm."

Some of this life and enthusiasm beamed back into the past when Mr. Melcher desired a name for the first medal and searched out that early publisher John Newbery. Newbery was the son of a farmer, but bookselling was in his ancestry. He was born in Berkshire, England, in 1713. Sixteen years later, having exhausted his interest in agriculture, as well as the reading material available at the farm, he attached himself to the printer William Carnan to learn the trade most natural to his taste. Now he was on the right path, and it ran straight. With the cheerful sagacity that was to mark all his endeavors, he some years later succeeded Carnan as owner of the business and husband of Carnan's widow.

However the history of children's books is told, the date 1744 stands out. In that year Mr. Newbery, thirty-one and in his prime, moved to London to enlarge upon his opportunities. His periodicals and patent medicines continued to flourish, but now he ventured at once into book publishing, the branch of his business which made his name memorable. Two hundred or more adult books and schoolbooks were to bear his imprint. However, during that year of his London debut John Newbery took another noteworthy step. He published his first book for children. Its title, which, Frederic Melcher once observed, has seldom since been surpassed in appeal, was *A Little Pretty Pocket Book*.

Indeed something wholly new was in progress at 65 St. Paul's Churchyard, Mr. Newbery's two-windowed book-shop at the sign of the Bible and Sun. Now it displayed the arresting notice: "Juvenile Library." To appreciate the value of these events, it is necessary to realize that there were no genuine children's books before this time, which is to say that there were no books designed to give children pleasure, without purpose to instruct or improve. Hornbooks and battledores had served long use, with better advantages to economy than to recreation. The little chapbooks had earned their niche from an eager public both old and young. John Newbery as a boy must have read many a penny's worth of this humble literature, and, like other English children, caught tempting first glimpses of a magic vista. Perhaps it was a longing whetted then that led the way to the real books which were to bear his name.

Children had not been overlooked entirely. There were of course old nursery rhymes, a few textbooks, the inevitable guides to conduct, and even Isaac Watts' *Divine and Moral Songs for Children,* published in 1715. Incidental scraps of fairy tales and *Aesop's Fables* fell in crumbs from the adult table. Young readers had claimed their rightful share in *Pilgrim's Progress, Robinson Crusoe,* and *Gulliver's Travels,* which had been written for their elders. But all this was without forethought or purpose. *A Little Pretty Pocket Book* in a single gesture announced that children had certain rights, and this first book which undertook merely to please them was there to prove it. Its flowered binding and gilt edges, and the carefully engraved little pictures, declared that young readers had found a friend.

Thus in 1744 did publishing for children make its modest beginning. In the second quarter of the twentieth century it was to become big business. To commemorate the two-hundredth anniversary of its tiny ancestor,

Frederic Melcher in 1944 had a facsimile of *A Little Pretty Pocket Book* printed from the rare American reprint. No copy of the first edition is known to exist. Libraries and collectors were happy to acquire this historic facsimile.

The Newbery firm passed to T. Carnan, then was owned by a nephew and named for him "Francis Newbery & Sons Ltd." Later it was possessed by other members of the long-lived family. It stood for one hundred and twenty-five years in St. Paul's Churchyard, then moved to Charterhouse Square, where it still carries on a patent-medicine business. It was uniquely linked to distant yet related scenes when Fenton Newbery, a great-grandson, fourth in direct descent from John, came from London to attend the American Library Association conference at Atlantic City in 1926, and saw the awarding of that year's Newbery Medal.

During his enthusiastic, energetic career John Newbery published about twenty books which, by today's standards, were genuine books for children. They contained little original material, but they freshened familiar nursery tales and rhymes by presenting them in their first nice dresses. Writers with suitable abilities were employed by Mr. Newbery to prepare the texts. They wrote new stories, too, when it was necessary.

Newbery's second and perhaps most expressive work was *The Lilliputian Magazine,* issued in one volume in 1752. Its varied contents included the popular adventures of "Tommy Trip and His Dog Jouler," and much besides, according to the subtitle: "The Young Gentleman and Lady's Golden Library, being an Attempt to mend the World, to render the Society of Man more Amiable, and to Establish the Plainness, Simplicity, Virtue and Wisdom of the Golden Age, so much celebrated by the Poets and Historians."

*Goody Two Shoes,* most famous and long-lasting of the Newbery publications, was practically the first original piece of English fiction written to entertain children. Its authorship is generally attributed to Oliver Goldsmith, but the fact cannot be established. *Mother Goose's Melody* achieved second place in fame. It was the first collection of English folk rhymes, and it used the term "Mother Goose" for the first time in English. Newbery borrowed that title from Perrault's *Contes de ma mère l'oie,* and it never returned to its origin, among French fairy tales.

Such inscriptions as "To all those who are good this book is dedicated by their best friend" are characteristic of John Newbery. He is described as amiable, generous, "the friend of all mankind." His bustling activities rushed him here and there, creating the memory of a man in a breathless flurry. Yet he could practice patience when young shoppers came to buy themselves a book and could not make up their minds. He sympathized with the restrained lives of Georgian children and crammed such assorted treats and indulgences into the pages of his books as the painfully proper times allowed.

John Newbery enjoyed twenty-three years of popularity and business success in London. He is portrayed sometimes as the patron saint of the new literature, other times as a very resourceful tradesman. Actually, of course, he was neither altogether, and both in part. Mr. Newbery was canny enough to realize that a large and eager market of young consumers awaited his wares, and that an accumulated store of nursery literature begged for decent publication. But his was no bargain merchandising. He lavished thoughtfulness upon each detail in his little books. Many were bound in thin Dutch paper, gilded and flowered, with the reds, golds, blues, and greens set in by hand. (As the covers aged they changed to mahogany brown.) Some of the illustrations were original, others were copied or recut from existing woodcuts. In spite of the care exercised in their making, these books were inexpensive, therefore available to people of ordinary income. Their format remains a mellow testimony to John Newbery. After he died, his son Francis wrote:

Few men have died more generally or more sincerely lamented. All the newspapers of the time spontaneously burst forth in expressions of commendations of his character, and of regret at his loss, which was considered as premature, as he was only fifty-four years of age. . . . He was scarcely ever seen without a book or pen in his hand, and his mind was ever occupied for some good purpose. . . . As, from the multiplicity of his concerns, he was apt to be forgetful of his engagements, the great author, Dr. Johnson, who had often ridiculed this propensity, made him the subject of one of his essays in "The Idler" under the humorous character of Jack Whirler.

(From Charles Welsh's *A Bookseller of the Last Century*.)

Newbery was not an educator. He was a benevolent bookseller. He saw that children's books could be important in his business, and he developed them with taste and enthusiasm. They proved by their success that they met a need. Above and beyond his printed works, John Newbery's genial example endures, living once each year in limelight that would overwhelm the old man—when the Newbery Medal is awarded in America to a distinguished book for children.

As companion award, the Caldecott Medal places beside publisher Newbery a fellow countryman whose artistic talent in a later period was to enliven the pages of many books. A full century after the birth of children's bookmaking, Randolph Caldecott was born on March 22, 1846, in Chester, England. His drawings were to recreate eighteenth-century scenes, reaching coincidentally back toward the Newbery period. Caldecott's span of life was only forty years, but his observations upon it, brimming from the pages of his picture books, would justify twice the time allotted him.

Children's books came a long way in the years between these two bookmen. They had passed after Newbery's time through travail, and near extinction, at the hands of the powerful moralists, and had at length reached more pleasant pastures.

In 1846, the year of Caldecott's birth, *Andersen's Fairy Tales* came out in their first English translation and *Lear's Nonsense Book* was published. By that time English editions of *Grimms' Fairy Tales* had circulated for two decades. George MacDonald, Thomas Hughes, Charles Kingsley, and Charlotte Yonge were currently widening the stream of literature for children. Clearly the recognition and value of this special literature had gained firm foothold. It was brilliantly illuminated in Caldecott's time by Robert Louis Stevenson, Lewis Carroll, Juliana Horatia Ewing, and on this side of the ocean by Mark Twain, Louisa May Alcott, and Mary Mapes Dodge. However, Caldecott's contemporaries in the graphic arts influenced his career more directly. They too were a distinguished company, including Walter Crane, Kate Greenaway, Sir John Tenniel, and Arthur Hughes. Illustration for children had come into its own in the Victorian era.

When he was fifteen Randolph Caldecott started work as a bank clerk, first in Whitchurch, Shropshire, then in Manchester. These jobs interfered only superficially with his hobbies of sketching, woodcarving, and modeling. In his wake at the bank were pictures scribbled on desk blotters and deposit slips. His true inclinations blossomed when he joined a Manchester artists' club, took lessons, and had sketches printed in the papers.

Hunting scenes, animal studies, and humor were the early staples of Caldecott's craft. In 1872 he moved to London, to a full-time artist's career. Leading magazines in England and the United States soon accepted his work. Caldecott's richer, deeper resources were revealed however when he made drawings for Washington Irving's *Old Christmas* and *Bracebridge Hall*. His mature talent retained all the humor, but he outgrew an early tendency to ridicule. His favorite subjects were children, country characters, horses, and dogs.

Photographs of Randolph Caldecott show a tall man with blond good looks which revealed in his face the fineness and sweetness of his nature. The vigor and joyousness of his drawings reflect the good spirits of a warmly spontaneous being. Like Robert Louis Stevenson, he possessed, alas, only this spiritual vitality. Both these men expressed themselves robustly and adventurously in everything they created, and thus belied the weakness of their physical frames. Caldecott's frail health often necessitated changes of climate. Book illustration suited his needs because it released him from the pressure of journalistic deadlines.

The great nineteenth-century color-printer Edmund Evans discovered Caldecott when he saw his illustrations for the Washington Irving stories. Evans was used to initiating ventures. With the perception that made his Racquet Court Press the inspiration and discipline of so many artists, from Walter Crane on, Evans called upon Caldecott to try his talents on a series of "toy" books for children. Thereupon, in 1878, Caldecott and Evans together produced *The House That Jack Built,* and *John Gilpin's Ride*. After their success, two picture books a year came forth regularly until 1885, when *The Great Panjandrum* ended the run. Eventually the sixteen picture books were bound in four volumes, and in this as in their original format enjoyed immense, highly profitable sales. The last product of this famous collaboration was the limited edition printed on large sheets, the rare Edition deLuxe dearly prized by collectors.

At the time of Evans' approach to Caldecott, Walter Crane was the outstanding picture-book artist in England. Caldecott consulted Crane before launching himself in the same field, and benefited ever after by Crane's friendship, encouragement, and praise. Two other staunch supporters of his work were women of creative talent, Kate Greenaway and Juliana Horatia Ewing. Caldecott and Miss Greenaway were twin illustrators, having been born in the same month and year. Caldecott met Mrs. Ewing while she was planning *The Story of Jackanapes,* and sketched for her a boy riding on a pony, before Lollo and Goose Green existed in written text. He interrupted his own picture-book schedule to illustrate several of Mrs. Ewing's stories.

Caldecott delighted in his ability to tell much in a few lines. "The fewer the lines the less error committed," was his modest creed. Being a great draftsman he did not have to rely upon color to tell his story. His method was to draw with pen and ink, then transfer his drawing to wood blocks for the engraving. He used a separate block for each of his colors, usually six. The beautiful color reproductions of Caldecott's work are due in large measure to the skilled craftsmanship and artistic sense of Edmund Evans.

The love and knowledge of country life, and his innate gaiety, never deserted Randolph Caldecott. His accurate memories, based upon a rural boyhood, and the drawings and models which were his earliest pastime bore their fruit in such universal favorites as *The Farmer's Boy, A Farmer Went Trotting upon His Grey Mare,* and *Three Jovial Huntsmen.* When you turn the pages of a Caldecott picture book you are in England. It is England on a sunny day with a wind blowing off the heath. The village streets, houses, and old stone walls stand deep-planted in their native earth. In fields and towns, people and animals trip, parade, chase, and run. Everything and everybody in the picture participate in it and add something to its liveliness.

All this tide of life and fun, the fence-jumping and the horn-blowing, the barking and crowing in the roadways, the courtly gestures, the puffing and racing, came to an untimely end in 1886. Caldecott, afflicted with tuberculosis, had traveled to Florida in search of sunshine but died in St. Augustine shortly afterward. The one-hundredth anniversary of his birth, and sixtieth of his death, were observed by the children's book world in 1946. Each year the imprint of his talent stands forth anew when the picture-book artist of the year accepts the Caldecott Medal.

Thus the three bookmen, Newbery, Caldecott, and Melcher, share the stage for a few moments annually. When the President of the Children's Services Division (of the American Library Association) presents the Newbery and Caldecott Medals to two happy winners, the ceremony is brief but its meaning is long. It points back to what has been accomplished and forward to the new talent, unseen and even unborn, that will emerge in its day.

# CHAPTER II

## *The Prior Scene*

Historically speaking, the literary climate was definitely favorable to a children's book award in 1921. Therefore some background of the times which produced the Newbery Medal seems an essential part of this account.

A great many good books for children could be found in the children's rooms of the public libraries in the early nineteen-twenties. There were enough of those older ones which had won continual use, and new ones were being written. But no strong, significant tides were moving. Like every other aspect of American life, children's books were ultimately affected, in their own way, by the First World War. An immediate aftermath was the influx of refugee authors and artists. Of course the influence of new European talent was not perceptible for a few years. Later on, warm new uses of color, combined with old world folklore and national traditions, would expand book horizons in this country.

There were other more immediate stirrings. The launching of Children's Book Week in 1919 indicated the rising vitality. Louise Seaman at the Macmillan Company became the first editor of children's books, in that same year. Three years later, in 1922, May Massee accepted a similar appointment with Doubleday, Page. These two events marked the beginning of genuine specialization in publishing for children. Meanwhile up in Boston in 1916 Bertha Mahony had brought into existence the first and most famous of the small, selective bookshops for children, under the auspices of the Women's Educational and Industrial Union. It was called the Bookshop for Boys and Girls, a name that acquired luster as the excellence of its Suggestive Purchase Lists attracted widening attention. These lists by Bertha Mahony and Elinor Whitney were parents of *The Horn Book* magazine. While their shop was demonstrating in Boston that literary standards could be put to daily use, Marian Cutter's bookshop for children took a corresponding position in New York.

These were authentic pulsations of the golden age in children's books that was dawning, and were fully related to the one further step which followed, the introduction of an award medal in children's literature.

Anne Carroll Moore in *My Roads to Childhood* (Horn Book, Inc.) provides a strikingly clear glimpse of the postwar literary condition, and proves that the ground was fertile for some fresh incentive to writers:

Conferences, individual and collective, with publishers and booksellers preceding the holidays of 1918 confirmed my faith that the time was ripe in America for a vigorous movement back to childhood and youth and their dramatic human interests. A number of publishers are eagerly looking for writers who have the power to communicate with children and young people on their own initiative. . . . I am convinced that publishers . . . really prefer authors who have ideas and the ability to express them, nor are they afraid to risk the work of unknown authors, provided it is good work. . . . We may as well face frankly at the outset this reluctance to write for children on the part of competent writers. . . . The present indications [in 1919] are that the number of outstanding books for children and young people will be smaller than for 1918. Several publishers have had a dreary winter and spring, two or three are childless, to their regret, but to our relief when we survey the variety of makeshifts and done-overs announced by others. We turn with a feeling of increased respect toward a house that has steadily declined manuscripts too poor for publication. There have been many such manuscripts in the market.

By 1920 work with children carried its well-understood share of public library service with practiced capability. The wartime dearth of librarians continued, however. Large library systems were conducting their own training classes, and were obliged to accept high-school graduates as apprentices, though of course preferring candidates with college education. Librarians inclined toward work in the children's rooms were quite generally put there without special schooling, but some of the leading library systems were able to offer in-service training in children's literature for staff members wishing to specialize in that direction.

Effie Power, superintendent of work with children in the Cleveland Public Library, found in 1921 and reported at the Swampscott Conference that "Careful scanning of the American Library Association membership shows one hundred ninety-six children's librarians," which was only four per cent of the total. Sixty-two of that number were graduates of the Carnegie Library School, then the chief training center. In the same address Miss Power appealed for better salaries, chances for advancement, and other material encouragements to young children's librarians. She said they had been overworked and their ranks depleted during the war, and the vacancies were not being filled. As chairman in 1921 of the A.L.A. Children's Librarians' Section (as it was then called), Clara W. Hunt, superintendent of work with children in the Brooklyn Public Library, sent a questionnaire to libraries to determine the potential strength of the Section. As a result she was able to list 472 librarians who preferred and supposedly were practicing, at least part of their library time, the work of children's librarian. Many of them obviously considered their designation as tentative, and had not felt involved with their professional organization.

It is not surprising that children's librarians, lacking force of numbers, were not yet assuming much leadership in setting standards for children's books. In this early postwar period there was great reliance upon those books which time and use had approved for young readers, and considerable timidity about any outright support, or public enthusiasm, for current productions. Anne Carroll Moore, superintendent of work with children in the New York Public Library, was the only recognized critic seriously appraising children's books for the press. Her reviews appeared in *The Bookman* from 1918 to 1927, and after 1924 her "Three Owls" page ran weekly in the *New York Herald Tribune* until 1930. Publication of Miss Moore's *Roads to Childhood* (later a part of *My Roads to Childhood*) in 1920 by Doubleday, Page was a milestone in literary criticism, and therefore in the progress of children's books. These had to gain more attention of press and public if they were to grow in numbers and importance. Current publications needed to engage more critical attention of librarians, as well.

Cornelia Meigs, Elsie Singmaster, Eliza Orne White, Lucy Fitch Perkins, and Caroline Dale Snedeker were prominent, familiar author names in the children's rooms in 1920. Boys were reading the Joseph Altsheler books, those by Ralph Henry Barbour, William Heyliger, Dillon Wallace. Three durable books published that year were Charles Boardman Hawes' first sea story *The Mutineers,* W. W. Tarn's *Treasure of the Isle of Mist,* and *The Story of Doctor Dolittle,* by Hugh Lofting. Padraic Colum was well known, but the imaginative arts of Walter de la Mare and Laurence Housman were more widely recognized a few years later, along with Carl Sandburg's *Rootabaga Stories.* Olaf Baker was the new teller of animal tales. His books were welcomed to freshen the shelves of well-worn Ernest Thompson Seton and Jack London volumes.

Every library owned and relied upon three twentieth-century fairy-tale classics: *The Magic Forest* by Stewart Edward White (1903), *The Wonderful Adventures of Nils* by Selma Langerlöf (1907), and *The Wind in the Willows* by Kenneth Grahame (1908). These library shelves were richly stored with collections of folk and fairy tales drawn from many lands, and with retellings from legends and mythology that formed the great literature of the past. Many of these retellings and translations set high standards, framing a lofty background for the new movements of the nineteen-twenties.

In realism too there was much looking backward in 1920. The stories by Howard Pyle, Robert Louis Stevenson, Rudyard Kipling, Mark Twain, and John Masefield enjoyed supreme status. Among home stories preferred by girls the old favorites by Louisa May Alcott, Laura E. Richards, Kate Douglas Wiggin, and Abbie Farwell Brown continued as popular as if they were the latest things. In the graphic arts, Boutet de Monvel, Leslie Brooke, Willebeek LeMair, and E. Boyd Smith had a strong hold upon the picture-book tastes, which also kept ties faithfully with Crane, Greenaway, and Caldecott.

This in brief was where children's books stood just after World War I, and just prior to the appearance on the scene of a brand new factor, the Newbery Medal.

# CHAPTER III

# *A Challenging Proposition*

"Never was there such a conference as this," said *Library Journal* of the 1921 American Library Association meeting at Swampscott, Massachusetts, which drew a record attendance of 1900 members. "Good measure, pressed down, shaken together and running over." It was the first library conference Frederic Melcher attended, but at that time, with three years with R. R. Bowker behind him, and being continually involved with libraries because of his work, he "had come to feel half librarian and half bookseller."

The first meeting of the Children's Librarians' Section was scheduled for June 21, with the chairman, Alice I. Hazeltine of the St. Louis Public Library, presiding. The theme, "Children's Book Week—A National Movement," was discussed from three points of view: by Frederic Melcher speaking for the National Association of Book Publishers, by Clara W. Hunt for librarians, and by Bertha Mahony for booksellers. "I remember that session very vividly," said Mr. Melcher more than thirty years later. As the Book Week national chairman he saw library support increasing as children's librarians discovered how well the idea fitted into their work, but there was still

35

something to be done to dispel the librarians' suspicions of "commercial taint."

The New Ocean House at Swampscott had no adequate auditorium, so the larger A.L.A. sessions met in a new unused garage, back of the hotel. The high platform presented speakers in a framework of steel beams. "There was a good audience, as measured by the registrations of the day," wrote Mr. Melcher. "It was a great opportunity for Book Week's promotion, and I was full of zeal caught from watching and serving children in bookstores for a quarter of a century. As I looked down from the platform at the three or four hundred people, I thought of the power they could have in encouraging the joy of reading among children. I could see that I was sure of having the librarians' cooperation in Children's Book Week, but I wanted to go further and secure their interest in the whole process of creating books for children, producing them, and bringing them to the children."

Mr. Melcher left that morning lamenting that the strong unity of purpose the meeting had built would melt away for another year when the conference ended and members returned to their own communities. He wished they would take home with them some solid, effective plan. He thought they were too timid in voicing their opinions of current efforts, and that as part of the literary trade they were absolutely obligated to go beyond selecting and distributing its products. He thought children's librarians should find ways to encourage the creation of more that was worth while, by writers of outstanding ability.

Amid this torrent of ideas, one crystallized in Melcher's

mind after that first session. The thought of an award, and a name for it, came to him suddenly. This was something that might be done. The second session was scheduled for the following afternoon. "I asked Miss Hazeltine if I might speak again. She gave me the time."

By chance Frederic Melcher had just been reading Charles Knight's *Shadows of Old Booksellers,* which had left on his mind a lively impression of John Newbery. *There* was the name to use in setting up such an award. What could be more appropriate than to honor the first bookseller who saw possibilities in publishing books particularly for children, the first to seek the right authors to write for them?

So, actually on the spur of the moment, the offer was proposed and a name for it suggested. A medal for children's books! Though ignored by Pulitzer and other adult literary prizes, here literature for the young opened itself to competition, exciting and untried.

Vital to the concept were these children's librarians gathered in Swampscott. Melcher saw them as "the jury which could give value to such an award and this was the time to inaugurate it, when ground swells of fresh interest in children's books were coming in from various directions." He chose children's librarians as best trustees of the prize, because their work had equal concern with all age levels. They brought together every kind of reader on equal footing, whereas parents and teachers were bound to their specified age groups.

The proposition so quickly built up in Melcher's mind was promptly applauded by the audience. They moved to put it into effect the next year. "A motion was made and carried that this be referred to the incoming officers to work out as they may think best with the approval of the Section," wrote the secretary.

The A.L.A. proceedings note other program features that occupied the afternoon. Alice M. Jordan, supervisor of work with children in the Boston Public Library, reported for the Book Production Committee that the manufacturing cost of books had grown to two and one-third times what it was before the war; that the cost of paper and cloth were decreasing, "but the labor situation tends to keep expenses high." Other leaders in library work with children, Elva S. Smith, Effie Power, Marian Cutter, Jean C. Roos, Julia Carter, Leonore Power, Lillian Smith, and Nina C. Brotherton took part in the afternoon program with papers and discussions.

However to those present the spontaneous proposal Mr. Melcher had injected during the meeting was the topic of paramount interest. Thirty-two years later Alice I. Hazeltine remembered the stir of conversation on the veranda after the meeting, as librarians discussed what had been said by that dynamic Mr. Melcher. Clara W. Hunt recalled the consensus promptly reached that if the award were already in effect, *The Story of Doctor Dolittle* would have been named the year's winner then and there.

To the Section's new officers elected at Swampscott fell all the unfamiliar tasks involved in organizing the new process of selecting the honor book. Clara W. Hunt, of the Brooklyn Public Library, became chairman, E. Gertrude Avey, Cincinnati Public Library, vice-chairman, and Leonore St. John Power, New York Public

Library, the secretary-treasurer. Only twenty-seven children's librarians paid their dues in 1921. That October the Section had on hand a balance of one dollar and ninety-five cents!

After the Swampscott conference the Executive Committee of the American Library Association took this new proposal under advisement, pending official action. The Section officers assumed its acceptance and discussed the first steps to be taken. Early in September Mr. Melcher wrote to Miss Hunt:

> I have wanted to put down on paper that I should be glad to go ahead and do my part if your Committee so desired, i.e., I will start immediately to find some method of providing for a medal to be awarded annually by the Section. I do not know at this writing how much the design would cost and how much the die would cost, but it would be my task to find some way to cover these items. Then the handling of the machinery of voting and all other matters are in your hands. . . .
>
> I should not imagine that there would be more than a half dozen books considered, though I may be wrong. There would probably have to be some specifications as to what books could be included, i.e., books published in the United States during the calendar year, perhaps; otherwise the voters might not feel informed to judge of books printed in other countries which they had not had reasonable opportunity to see, and few books in foreign languages get over here in sufficient quantity to be considered.

Mr. Melcher had reached an early conclusion that the award might well be a medal, as a money award would require a large capital sum. The children's librarians' seal of approval would reward the author, and the inevitable increment to the book's sale would be a satisfaction to both author and publisher.

That winter the Section officers gave thought to many questions confronting them. First, who was entitled to cast ballots for the competing books? Membership in the Section was defined thus: "Active or voting members shall consist of library assistants whose entire time is given to work with children in libraries and schools, and librarians and assistants who are actively representing work with children." Many of these were not yet listed on the Section rolls.

Next question: Who would make the final decision? "It is most important that the final judges of the award be a few of the people of recognized high standards and experience," Miss Hunt wrote her vice-chairman. "If a majority vote of all so-called children's librarians determines the award it is entirely possible for a mediocre book to get the medal. To give everybody a chance to make nominations will create interest and induce good feeling. The publicity of this thing will be great for children's books."

Soon the *Library Journal* and other professional magazines carried notices of the award idea and invited nominations for the best children's book published in the United States in 1921. A letter went to each of the nearly five hundred practicing children's librarians, urging them to enroll in the Section and attend the next conference. It was judged, and rightly, that the first presentation of the Newbery Medal offered a decided attraction. "The idea of urging attendance at the next A.L.A. is splendid," wrote Miss Avey. "If we begin to talk about this now I am sure children's librarians will plan to go as soon as they hear where we are to meet."

In case of a close popular verdict, it was decided that final choice of the winning book would be left to a jury composed of the officers and four other leading children's librarians: Alice Jordan of Boston, Mrs. Mary E. S. Root of Providence, Anne Carroll Moore of New York, and Effie Power of Cleveland. Nominations were due on March 1, and all librarians, not only children's librarians, were invited to take part.

When Miss Hunt submitted drafts of the announcements for the magazines to Mr. Melcher in December he answered, "I think you will permit me to write my name a little smaller into the plan and to let it stand more specifically as an A.L.A. function. I made the suggestion as a member of the American Library Association, interested that the full potential value of its professional standards should be available in every possible way." He went on to reaffirm that "the creative genius which serves children's interests deserves public appreciation as much as creative genius in other fields. . . . I suppose that it might be considered true that more painstaking thought is given to the children's books in this country than in any other. A painstaking book does not mean a work of genius, but it is a step in the right direction, and out of the pains taken will arrive the books of genius which we want to award. . . . I have been talking with a sculptor who has been highly recommended, and am waiting for a further conference with him. My suggestion to him was that what we wanted to reward was 'genius giving of its best to the child.' "

# CHAPTER IV

# *The First Newbery Medal*

By March 8, 1922, librarians' replies to the invitation asking them to help nominate the first Newbery Medal book could be tabulated. Two hundred and twelve votes had been received. The top six books were:

| | | |
|---|---|---|
| Hendrik Willem Van Loon | *Story of Mankind* | 163 votes |
| Charles Boardman Hawes | *The Great Quest* | 22 " |
| Bernard Marshall | *Cedric the Forester* | 7 " |
| William Bowen | *Old Tobacco Shop* | 5 " |
| Padraic Colum | *The Golden Fleece* | 4 " |
| Cornelia Meigs | *Windy Hill* | 2 " |

Nine other titles received one vote each. The verdict being unmistakable, no work was left for the Award Jury. In a letter sent to each jury member late in March, Miss Hunt said, "Mr. Melcher is so anxious to have the name of the winning author absolutely not known until the day of the award that, since there were no complications for our 'Jury' to straighten out I promised him I would not tell a soul except himself. . . . Now please don't guess aloud! Men think women can't keep a secret. Let's prove to Mr. Melcher that we can." Therein was set a pattern, or code of practice, that lasted for twenty-seven years. Keeping the secret was from the beginning a matter of honor.

The young sculptor René Paul Chambellan had been engaged by Mr. Melcher to design the Medal. Several public buildings in New York already showed the work of Chambellan, and in the spring of 1922 he was busy making the series of large sculptured panels for the Russell Sage Foundation building. Letters in the Melcher files, current with the completion of the Medal, reflect the admiration of those who were allowed a preview of it before the approaching June conference of the A.L.A., scheduled in Detroit.

On the Medal, handsomely struck in bronze, a central figure and two youthful ones represent the writer giving his imaginative talents to the children.

"The reason I have been rather averse to having my name much connected [with the award] is because someone might think this was a book campaign or publishers' idea, and I would like to have my part in it entirely personal," Frederic Melcher wrote Miss Hunt at about this time. "The enthusiasm for the plan is not that of the Secretary of a Publishers' Association, but that of one

who has been close to the distribution of children's books
for twenty-five years and besides that a parent of three
children. I cannot quite separate my name from the campaign connection, but for that reason would rather John
Newbery bear with the American Library Association the
brunt of the publicity."

The June date for the annual A.L.A. meeting was now
at hand. Shortly before leaving for Detroit Mr. Melcher
wrote Miss Hunt, "It would seem to me that, if I am to
be part of the ceremony, as seems to be suggested by the
convention program, the process should be that I would
turn over to you, as Chairman of the Children's Section,
the Medal as a continuing and permanent institution, and
then you would present it as this year's award to the
winner. After we have had this first presentation, I will
want to put in writing for the records of your Section of
the American Library Association full statement of my
agreement to see that the Medal is struck off each year,
with the understanding that it is always to be in the hands
of the Children's Section or of the American Library
Association for presentation, some record so that there
cannot be any misunderstanding."

The Detroit conference opened on June 26, 1922. The
A.L.A. Proceedings record that "The first meeting of the
Children's Librarians' Section was held Tuesday afternoon, June 27th, with Clara W. Hunt, Chairman, presiding. This session was devoted to the general subject of
the book itself discussed in various phases." There were
papers by Margaret B. Carnegie, of the Carnegie Library,
Pittsburgh, Anne I. M. Jackson and Marion F. Schwab,
of the Brooklyn Public Library, Elizabeth D. Briggs,

Cleveland Public Library, and Mary S. Wilkinson, of the Hackley Public Library, Muskegon, Michigan. "The culmination of the first session," continue the Proceedings, "was the awarding of the first John Newbery Medal for the most distinguished contribution to American literature for children during the year 1921 to Dr. Hendrik Willem Van Loon for *The Story of Mankind*. Clara Whitehill Hunt, Chairman, accepted the medal from Frederic G. Melcher, on behalf of the Children's Librarians' Section, and then presented it to Dr. Van Loon who made a very appreciative speech to the large audience who had come to witness the presentation."

We are told that the hall was indeed full to capacity, and many were turned away. Miss Hunt could see in her memory, after full thirty years, a long narrow room with windows down the side, and the crowded seating. When Mr. Melcher handed the Medal to her she replied, "I would I had the ability to express adequately the gratitude which we children's librarians feel for the inspiration which prompted you to make this gift to the cause we love. . . . We feel strong and powerful because you believe in us and are putting in our hands a weapon, one of the most potent of our times—publicity of the best kind." Miss Hunt then presented the Medal to Dr. Van Loon. As soon as possible afterward the three stars of this ceremony were hustled down to the sidewalk for pictures and a newsreel recording. Van Loon's name attracted great notice because of the popularity of his book with adult readers, so he gave the award a conspicuous debut.

When the Section's next session convened, the following day, Mrs. Mary E. S. Root, who organized children's library work in Providence, Rhode Island, "opened the meeting with a delightful paper, 'Chartered Seas,' in which she described how children's library work had grown since the organization of a Children's Librarians' Section of the American Library Association in 1901. She spoke of the 'little ship which was the children's library movement twenty-one years ago,' and paid tribute to the early pilots who kept the venturesome craft on its course. 'Appreciation has come,' said Mrs. Root. 'The pilot of today whose good judgment was looked upon with distrust in the past must travel early and late if she would begin to meet the demands made upon her for lectures on children's books before mothers' clubs, library clubs, library schools, and summer schools. She must go sleepless if she would prepare all the lists asked of her. She must check the *Booklist* and other cooperative lists, and, crowning triumph in the year of Our Lord, 1922, she awards the John Newbery Medal for the most distinguished juvenile published this year.' "

Among the resolutions passed at the subsequent business meeting of the Section, this one concludes the history of the first award:

Be it resolved that we as members of the Children's Librarians' Section of the American Library Association express to Mr. Frederic G. Melcher our gratitude for originating the idea of the John Newbery Medal, an award which should be of real service to the cause of children's literature in determining a future standard of excellence of workmanship and a spirit which will correspond to the ideals for which we are working.

We are especially honored because he has conferred upon

us a perpetual trust of selecting the future literature which shall receive the award. And lastly, we appreciate the generosity which prompted the gift and saw it executed in so beautiful and worthy a fashion.

Perhaps the most suitable words were penned by Frederic Melcher himself, just a month later. In the *Publishers' Weekly* of July 22, 1922, he said, "We should not forget that by creating a greater audience, we are also creating literature itself, for the creator of literature is drawn out by the appreciation of literature, the author needs the audience as much as the audience needs the author."

# CHAPTER V

## *Mastery of the Selection Process*

There remained to be framed the necessary formal agreements between Frederic Melcher and the American Library Association for the continued presentation of the annual Newbery Medal. On November 9, 1922, Mr. Melcher as donor forwarded to Carl H. Milam, A.L.A. secretary, a full statement of the Medal's origin and intent, for the information of the A.L.A. Executive Board. The statement read as follows:

THE JOHN NEWBERY MEDAL: Established in 1921 as an annual award for "the most distinguished contribution to American literature for children."

*Donor:* Frederic G. Melcher of New York.

*Sculptor:* René Chambellan of New York.

*Awarded by:* The Children's Librarians' Section of the American Library Association or the specialists in children's work in the American Library Association, under whatever name they may be organized.

*The Medal:* The donor agrees to have struck each year at his expense one bronze medal from the dies, and to have this engraved with the winner's name and the year covered by the award, and to place it in case ready for presentation by the librarians, and to deliver it to the responsible authorities in the Library Association at time designated by them. Or his heirs will undertake to do the same. The steel dies are at this date (November, 1922) deposited for safe-keeping with the Medallic Art Company, 137 East 29th Street, New York City, and may be taken from there, according to instructions filed with them, by the donor or by executive head of the American Library Association. The original sculpture remains with the donor for appropriate disposition.

*The Recipient of the Award:* The medal is to be awarded annually to the author of the "most distinguished contribution to American literature for children," the award being made to cover books whose publication in book form falls in the calendar year last elapsed. The award is restricted to authors who are citizens or residents of the United States. Reprints and compilations are not eligible for consideration. There are no limitations as to the character of the book considered except that it be original work. It need not be written solely for children, the judgment of the librarians voting shall decide whether a book be a "contribution to the literature for children." The award considers only the books of one calendar year and does not pass judgment on the author's previous work or other work during that year outside the volume that may be named.

*The Method of Award:* The donor agrees to leave the methods and practice of selecting each annual winner of the John Newbery Medal entirely to the American Library Association, whose president shall have power to delegate each year the responsibility for all details to the officers of a subsidiary group in the Association. It is the thought of the donor that the decision should be made by votes of such members of the American Library

Association as are especially connected with the work with children or with young people. If the award be announced at the annual meeting of the American Library Association, the months between January first and that date will be available for process of election. It may be possible to have the author present at the annual conference to receive the award then first announced; otherwise the name might be there announced and proper delegate appointed to deliver same.

*Possible Termination of Arrangement:* The American Library Association may terminate its agreement to serve as the awarding body by two-thirds vote of its Executive Board. Such decision to be communicated to the donor before October 1 of any year. The donor or heirs may terminate the agreement by three years' notice to the American Library Association or may endow the award with funds sufficient to cover costs of striking, engraving, and case, leaving the medal thereafter entirely in the hands of the American Library Association.

*The Purpose of the John Newbery Medal:* To encourage original and creative work in the field of books for children. To emphasize to the public that contributions to the literature for children deserve recognition as do poetry, plays, or novels. To give to those librarians who make it their life work to serve children's reading interests, an opportunity to encourage good writing in this field.

*The Name of Newbery:* The donor has connected the name of John Newbery with this award. This lovable bookseller and publisher of the eighteenth century, London, was perhaps the first bookman to appreciate that the reading interests of children were worthy of especial and individual attention.

The Executive Board, meeting at the Hotel Sherman in Chicago on December 27, voted to "accept Mr. Melcher's offer and assume the responsibility for the Medal, assigning to the Children's Librarians' Section the selection of the recipient." (As further rulings were framed by the Section, to clarify proceedings, they were added to the official contract, and will be recorded here in their chronological place.)

A few inevitable early wrinkles were soon ironed out. There were immediate questions from influential children's librarians as to the extent of Section authority. "My first agreement was with the Children's Section," Mr. Melcher wrote Mr. Milam, "but as that is not an organized group, I think the A.L.A. should be responsible and that the president can delegate the details to this Children's Section, and, in case there should be reorganization, some similar group could take the responsibility."

Several exchanges of letters on this point yielded an agreement satisfactory to Section officers that the A.L.A. would allow the children's librarians both the freedom and the power they thought necessary. An additional clause amended the original Melcher statement, according to A.L.A. Executive Board minutes: "Voted: That the book selected by vote of the members of the Children's Librarians' Section shall be the book for which the John Newbery Medal is awarded."

Miss Elva S. Smith of the Carnegie Library, Pittsburgh, was chairman of the Section in 1923. She wrote to the membership in January about choosing, for the second time, a Newbery award book: "A high standard of merit must be maintained, if the award is to serve its purpose of stimulating interest in real literature for children. May I, therefore, emphasize the personal responsibility of every children's librarian for a careful and discriminating choice. On account of the early date set for the conference, all votes should be in the hands of the chairman of the Children's Librarians' Section not later than March 1, 1923."

This round of voting resulted in the selection of Hugh Lofting's *Voyages of Doctor Dolittle* as the next winner. Some revision of the method was now contemplated. The Book Evaluation Committee, reporting for 1923-24, said, "The method of award of the Newbery Medal does not seem satisfactory. We do not believe that a popular vote of the Section can be depended upon to select the most distinguished contribution for the year and think another method should be devised."

This other method emerged from the A.L.A. conference at Saratoga Springs in 1924. Sixty-seven of the Section's members, who numbered 198 children's librarians at the time, had registered and among other things had seen the third Newbery honor go to *The Dark Frigate* by Charles Boardman Hawes. At the business meeting Effie L. Power offered the resolution that would constitute a special award committee, consisting of the Section's Executive Board and all members of the Book Evaluation Committee. Further discussion brought out the desirability of a slightly larger group. Alice Hazeltine proposed that three members-at-large be elected by the Section. This went into effect, with the immediate election of Mary Gould Davis of the New York Public Library, Enid Endicott of Toronto, and Louise Latimer of Washington, D.C., filling out the new Award Committee. All these moves were embodied in a resolution adopted at Saratoga Springs by the A.L.A. Executive Board, which further stated that "the award shall be communicated to the Executive Board of the American Library Association before the public announcement at the annual meeting when the award is made."

About the time of this 1924 conference Mr. Melcher in summarizing Medal affairs to date wrote, "Already the significance of this attention to books suitable for children has been noticed. There has been comment on the award from all parts of the country and there has been very general acceptance that this emphasis on new books for children will have a constructive effect in encouraging further books of value."

When the nineteen-twenties had run their course, five more authors had been honored: Charles J. Finger, Arthur Bowie Chrisman, Will James, Dhan Gopal Mukerji, and Eric P. Kelly. The business of selecting the award-winning book had been absorbed into the Section's basic schedule. In 1929 the children's librarians revised their constitution and voted to rename their organization the Section for Library Work with Children. Among the new provisions the Newbery Committee was enlarged to fifteen, through a redefinition of the Section's Executive Board. It would consist hereafter of the four current officers, the ex-chairman, and the chairmen of the standing committees. The membership ranks were growing and the wide-ranging activities undertaken by committees of children's librarians were making the nineteen-twenties their most progressive and fruitful decade.

Assuredly the prestige of the Newbery Medal was steadily increasing. Section members were still invited to send in suggestions for the most deserving book, but these were not binding upon the committee that made the choice. We see that in 1928 only 150 popular votes were received. It had become a committee affair. The actual presentation, however, was enjoyed by librarians from all walks. Naturally the occasion had become the most conspicuous feature of the Section's conference schedule. By the end of the decade the annual reports indicate that the phrase "The culmination of the meeting was the awarding . . ." had become stock property of the various secretaries.

Children's librarians at the American Library Association convention in Washington, D.C., May 1929, noted a twenty-five-per-cent increase in children's books published, over 1925. "Publishers are more conscious than formerly of securing the approval of children's librarians and the A.L.A.," reports the secretary's minutes. "The presentation by Miss [Carrie E.] Scott of the medal for the John Newbery Award to Eric P. Kelly for his *Trumpeter of Krakow* was the culmination of this meeting. The applause that attended the announcement of the winner showed the choice to be heartily endorsed by those present."

# CHAPTER VI

# *The Widening Scope*

Memories of the 1930 conference of the American
Library Association, when children's librarians honored
Rachel Field, have been recalled by Effie L. Power,
who was the Section's chairman that year. The famous little wooden doll Hitty was coming to Los An-
geles by airplane with Miss Field. "The fun began for
us when her publisher's representative arranged for a
group to meet Miss Field at the airport on her arrival. In
those days the airport was small and not crowded. Part
of the group went out to meet her in a chartered plane.
Others stayed on the ground to greet her in case her plane
landed first," wrote Miss Power in February 1954. There
was extraordinary interest in Rachel Field, so the presentation of the Newbery Medal was to be staged at the last
General Session on Saturday of conference week, in order
that the whole A.L.A. assembly could attend. "When
Saturday morning arrived," continues Miss Power, "the
precious medal was locked so securely in my trunk that
I had to call a mechanic to rescue it. But I arrived in
time with our guest, to find our officers and those of the
School Librarians' Section whom we had invited to share

honors with us, seated on the platform before a large audience." The new decade began thus auspiciously.

The nineteen-thirties set definite trends in children's books. Looking back we see clearly that they bore their own witness to a unique era. The country was gripped by a general depression, yet book production accelerated. The job of book selection began to overwhelm children's librarians, as the publication lists competed for length, and books of slight value crowded the better ones for space. Standardization and commercialization, unhealthy twins of the period, raised their ugly young heads. They indicated new trends in the children's book business, and soon loomed large and fixed in the general scene. But there were more heartening influences at work, to weight the scales against increasing pressures of mass production. One compensating weight was the remarkable rise of stories with European or other foreign backgrounds that built a new internationalism in American children's books. If the result of this was a dearth of stories about American life, then the few published were regarded more appreciatively. Emphasis upon good bookmaking grew rapidly in this decade, bringing fine picture books and illustrations to the fore, as the capabilities of new color-printing processes were explored by artists. Books for little children increased and took on variety, and non-fiction writing improved in quality and range.

Newbery awards during the nineteen-thirties reflect several of these trends. There was solid American bed-rock in such books as *Hitty, Waterless Mountain, Invincible Louisa, Caddie Woodlawn, Roller Skates,* and *Thimble Summer.* These were dearly prized in the boom time of tourist-made fiction, which brought back home for quick use every setting within reach of ship or plane, to supply our reading lists with "stories of other lands." Too many of them were hurriedly written, out of scant knowledge and little imagination. On the other hand this international spirit bore worthy laurels, with acclaim by children's librarians for *The Cat Who Went to Heaven, Young Fu of the Upper Yangtze, Dobry,* and *The White Stag.* Many of these winners were handsome examples also of the regenerated graphic arts.

Questions of eligibility arose from time to time as new kinds of books were considered for the prize, and led to two rulings which became part of the permanent code for the awards, at the New Orleans conference in April 1932. The first had been worded by Elva S. Smith:

To be eligible for the Newbery Medal books must be original, or, if traditional in origin, the result of individual research, the retelling and reinterpretation being the writer's own.

Then the Section adopted this further resolution, and both were approved by the A.L.A. Executive Board:

Since the Newbery Medal is intended to encourage an increasing number of authors to devote their best efforts to creating children's literature, the book of a previous recipient of the Newbery Medal shall receive the award only upon unanimous vote of the Newbery Committee.

This was rescinded in 1958, as no longer necessary. Joint authors were made eligible by a 1963 ruling.

Award committees with unflagging conscientiousness tried to improve upon methods used by their predecessors,

In 1933 the chairman, Della McGregor of St. Paul, Minnesota, invited twenty-five publishers to submit three to five names of their top new books for children. The members felt it was time to prove to the publishers that the librarians were completely open-minded, and possessed of every intention of considering all candidates. These committee members afterward stated that no pressure was brought by any publisher as a result of the experiment. (The committee of course considered many books besides those suggested in reply.) This procedure however was not formally repeated because it did not expedite the committee's work. Murmurings for the popular vote arose periodically, and the membership was urged continuously to send in all expressions of choice. By 1934 the winner was decided on points, as members of the committee sent first, second, and third preferences to the chairman. *Invincible Louisa,* for example, received eleven of fifteen firsts, and four seconds in the tabulation, for a close to maximum score.

Editors of children's books were employed in the leading houses by 1930, and their number grew until the depression made its mark upon book-trade personnel. Most of them regularly attended American Library Association conferences. As they and the children's librarians learned to discuss their ideas and problems together, a beneficial cooperation developed. Oldtimers on both sides could look back with amusement at earlier library fears of "commercial contamination." At the Montreal conference in 1934, May Massee, then editor of children's books at Doubleday, Doran, challenged children's librarians to stop fearing and distrusting those who had books to sell, because the editors too were trying to do a worthwhile job for children.

Still trying to widen membership participation in the awards, the Section next provided printed forms on which nominations were made along with payment of dues. The Newbery Committee necessarily considered every book nominated, so there was assurance that none was overlooked. In a move to seal off leaks identifying the winning title, the chairman, after 1933, no longer reported to committee members the result of the final votes. With only Mr. Melcher, the publisher, and author notified, the secret was known to the fewest possible, and the suspense was heightened. From voting time until the annual conference every year the Newbery choice was an unfailing subject for conjecture and conversation when children's book people met. Each year the announcement of the winner stood out as a major attraction at the A.L.A. meeting. The records mention that two thousand heard the address of Elizabeth Foreman Lewis at Chicago when she received the Medal in 1933.

Informal social affairs—luncheons and teas—had been connected with several earlier awards, but on October 18, 1933, the first "award dinner" was held at the Stevens Hotel in Chicago, under the chairmanship of Della McGregor. In 1936 a dinner again was staged, and in 1937 its fame was established. That year, with the American Library Association meeting in New York, the dinner at the Hotel Pierre honored Ruth Sawyer as author of *Roller Skates*. Mrs. Eleanor Roosevelt, the guest speaker, wrote in her newspaper column about it, "The speeches were short and good, but the crowning event of the evening was the Irish story told by Miss Sawyer. She said her nurse Joanna said it was a grand story 'to put manners on children,' but I am not at all sure it wasn't just as good a story for all of us grown-ups." By 1938 children's librarians were alluding to their "annual dinner" and in 1939 it was first officially recorded as a "banquet." That year, in San Francisco, the awards paraded in hitherto unmatched festivities. Ever since, during conference week, the footlights have been turned on one night for children's books, to bring together medal winners, publishers, children's and school librarians, and their guests.

In all awarding of book prizes, unanimous enthusiasm for a candidate is rare. Inevitably criticisms arose, here and there, that children themselves did not like many of the Newbery books, and that their preferences should be more seriously considered. The issue stirred up charges and countercharges among children's librarians, without, however, reaching wide-scale proportions at any time. Criticism of a Newbery Committee for its decision could not be sustained, because each year its members changed. They were children's librarians from all parts of the country, an unaided jury, presumably taking into account, insofar as they cared to do so, the young readers' viewpoints which were available to them daily and abundantly. Section leaders realized that the cumulative value of the Newbery Medal was at stake in these discussions. Letters, published articles, minutes of meetings dealt seriously with the whole contention. The responsibility for the Medal was never held lightly. Were the award books too literary? too old in appeal? Were some indeed read more by the high-school ages? Were they running too much to the girls' side? Where were the strong, red-blooded books for boys? These questions pressed for answers. Yet in 1936 Mr. Melcher found that "the technique of the Section must have been good, or there would not be so much general satisfaction."

The year 1937 brought two noteworthy developments. One of these was the establishment of a second award, the Caldecott Medal, for the artist who created the most distinguished picture book. This story will be told in the next chapter.

In the other development the school librarians came to be included in the committee that hereafter would select both prize-winning books. This latter event was directly related to the introduction of the companion award. When the Caldecott Medal proposal was sent to the A.L.A. Executive Board for ratification, it furnished a suitable opportunity to review the Newbery Medal's original authorization, and the procedures developed up to that time. "It is the thought of the donor that the decision should be made by votes of such members of the American Library Association as are especially connected with the work with children or young people," Frederic Melcher had stated in the 1922 agreement. During the fifteen years since, the School Libraries Section had grown and taken in many more members working with the elementary grades. The school librarians were regularly invited to attend the meeting at which the Newbery Medal was presented, but they had no other connection with the affair. Increasing cooperation was hoped for between children's and school librarians, two groups with similar training, serving the same readers.

The Medal awards provided natural and pleasant meeting ground for their common interests, as well as an association that would widen the base of selection.

The children's librarians discussed this potential enlargement of the award committee at their business meeting during the 1937 A.L.A. conference in New York. These resolutions resulted: "That the School Libraries Section be invited to take part in the Newbery and Caldecott Awards" and "That the chairman of the School Libraries Section and four other school librarians designated by the Section be given votes for the Newbery and Caldecott Awards and that these five persons be added to the Award Committee."

The School Libraries Section accepted the invitation, and ruled that four members be appointed annually to join their chairman as members of the Award Committee. This brought the Committee up to twenty-three members, for with the addition of chairmen of three new standing committees (Membership, Publicity, and International) the children's librarians involved now numbered eighteen. That year, 1937, the children's librarians could count 797 members in their Section. Again it was stressed to these members, and also to members of the Schools Section, that nominations for the medal books were desired from all ranks.

Viewing the accomplishments of that busy year, it seems proper now to conclude that the medal scheme had reached maturity.

# CHAPTER VII

# The Caldecott Medal

Rumors of an additional medal, to honor picture books, were abroad in the land by 1936. Actually the idea had been simmering in Frederic Melcher's mind for quite a time before that, and was supported by spokesmen for children's librarians. The brilliant work of picture-book artists in the nineteen-thirties needed full critical attention, and wider acclaim where it was deserved. It demanded recognition equal to that which authorship enjoyed. Everyone agreed too that younger children's books had not fared well in competing for the Newbery Medal. There was this difference of opinion: would a second medal serve the best interests, or would it detract from the prestige of the Newbery Medal? In May 1936 the Section Chairman, Jessie E. Tompkins of Detroit, wrote Mr. Melcher that her Award Committee heartily favored the new medal possibility. Mr. Melcher replied that he would cooperate if, "in the careful judgment of the committee, such an award would be of supplementary interest."

The incoming officers and committee members for 1937 considered the proposal and gave their unanimous consent. Mr. Melcher meantime had thought things

63

through, and had chosen Randolph Caldecott as the artist whose memory could be most appropriately honored, if a picture-book medal came into existence.

"The advantage of the word 'Caldecott,'" he wrote Muriel Gilbert, Buffalo Public Library, the incoming chairman, in March 1937, "is not only that it has pleasant connotations for everyone, but . . . [his work] was very definitely the kind of thing where the interest was in the pictures, yet there never was a book where the text was inconsequential. It would be my impulse to say that we should include in the wording of the final statement that we suggest that the books be judged by the pictures but that the text should be worthy of the pictures. It would be specified that the text would not of necessity be fresh material, that it would have to be in English, and the book, as with the Newbery Medal book, would have to be manufactured here."

When the American Library Association convened in New York in June, this was a feature item on the business-meeting agenda for the Section. The minutes record that on June 24, 1937, in the ballroom of the Waldorf-Astoria, the children's librarians "accepted with enthusiasm the generous offer of Frederic G. Melcher. . . ." They passed the following resolution:

Resolved: That the Picture Book Medal offered by Mr. Frederic G. Melcher be accepted. The name of this medal shall be the Caldecott Medal. This medal shall be awarded to the artist of the most distinguished American Picture Book for Children published in the United States during the preceding year. The award shall go to the artist, who must be a citizen or resident of the United States, whether or not he be the author of the text. Members of the Newbery Medal Committee will serve as judges. If a book of the year is nominated for both the Newbery and Caldecott awards, the Committee shall decide under which heading it shall be voted upon, so that the same title shall not be considered on both ballots.

This resolution and its concurrent one, which brought the School Librarians into the Awards Committee, were approved by the A.L.A. Executive Board two days later.

Soon after the conference ended Frederic Melcher set down his reasons for naming the new medal for Randolph Caldecott. "First: we should not use the name of a living person. Secondly: in the history of the picture book Caldecott has an important place. Thirdly: it supplies us with a name that has pleasant memories—memories connected with the joyousness of picture books as well as with their beauty. Whatever direction new books may take, I think that joyous and happy approach is one thing we should be gently reminded of."

Mr. Melcher was ready in the near future to consider a design for the Caldecott Medal. Not surprisingly he returned to Chambellan, who by 1937 was well known for his work on the low-relief sculpture in Rockefeller Center. Here is a Melcher account of what happened next: "I gave the sculptor, René Chambellan, a collection of Caldecott's books, not specifying that the Caldecott designs should be used, but wishing him to understand the spirit of Caldecott and the reasons for his continuing value. Mr. Chambellan became so delighted with Caldecott's draftsmanship that he immediately said he could do nothing better than put a few of the typical scenes on the medal, and this he has done."

The sculptor happily captured the spirit of John Gilpin taking his famous ride, for the face of the Medal. The other side pictures the pie, containing four-and-twenty blackbirds, being set before the king.

The beauty of the new Medal immediately gratified its beholders. The first strike in bronze from the dies was delivered to Mr. Melcher in December 1937. He took it directly to Chicago to give the A.L.A. midwinter meeting a preview. Space remained for engraving the name of the owner-to-be, which was not yet so much as a scratch on a ballot.

The Section for Library Work with Children proceeded easily with the votes for the first Caldecott award book. The machinery which had been tested and improved by sixteen Newbery Medal selections was ready. So, rather than problems, there was only an enlivening new interest for the Award Committee.

The early committees did need admonishment to distinguish between illustrated books and picture books. The initiative and dominant feature must be the work of the artist, Mr. Melcher wrote the chairman, in reply to questions expectedly raised.

In Kansas City on June 14, 1938, Julia Carter of the Cincinnati Public Library presented the first Caldecott Medal to Dorothy P. Lathrop, for her distinguished picture book *Animals of the Bible*. Randolph Caldecott, who with Walter Crane and Kate Greenaway had brought in the new age of the picture book, was recaptured in the affections of book lovers everywhere. His gay, vigorous spirit had earned and won a fresh lease of life.

# CHAPTER VIII

## *The Awards in Their Maturity*

One indication of the growth of a subject is the increase and weight of folders that accumulate, bulge, divide, and subdivide in that noble installation, the office filing cabinet. Folders by the pound and folders by the drawerful have furnished facts for this brief history. Mere physical dimensions of the material tell a great deal about the Newbery and Caldecott Medals, from their uncomplicated beginnings to their present diverse affairs. The swelling bulk of letters, clippings, schedules, releases, and radio and television scripts are all a part of the maturing process, and of changing times.

Before the procedure was altered in 1949, an established routine which is now part of the historical record had been inherited by the continuous line of Section (later, C.L.A.) chairmen. (The Section for Library Work with Children became the Children's Library Association, of the Division of Libraries for Children and Young People, in 1941, when reorganization of the American Library Association went into effect. New Division by-laws adopted in 1958 made it the Children's Services Division. These steps formerly were standard practice, upon completion of voting for the annual awards:

68

C.L.A. vice-chairman (as chairman of Newbery-Caldecott Committee) informs C.L.A. chairman of ballot results.

C.L.A. chairman notifies Frederic Melcher and A.L.A. Public Relations Office.

Melcher notifies the publishers of the two winning books, in strict privacy.

Chairman officially notifies the winners, with cautions of secrecy.

Winners prepare acceptance speeches and remarks for broadcast.

A.L.A. prepares publicity, for release to five hundred newspapers, magazines, organizations, and library presses, on announcement day.

C.L.A. chairman arranges for full-length copies of acceptance speeches to be sent to *The Horn Book* magazine.*

Vice-chairman writes article on awards for July *A.L.A. Bulletin.*

A.L.A. Publicity office arranges for photographs and interviews.

C.L.A. chairman makes conference plans for entertaining winners.

The Children's Services Division president and vice-president each year inherit duties requiring extraordinary diligence. The awards of course are but one of many undertakings, but the myriad details of their selection and presentation demand and deserve scrupulous attention. The reader of these redoubtable file cases is bound to be

---

* The collected speeches of Newbery and Caldecott authors, with critical and descriptive material on the books, have been published in two volumes by The Horn Book, Inc. (*Newbery Medal Books: 1922–1955* and *Caldecott Medal Books: 1938–1957*).

impressed by what has been done, in its total mass: the letters written, hundreds upon hundreds, to explain, to harmonize, sometimes even to search the soul. Librarians, a literate clan, seldom spare their pens. These are idealistic letters, as good, sound, and wise as their writers' sincere intentions. The welfare of the profession is their genuine concern. The full history of the Medals must pay homage to the letters which have nurtured them, the massive correspondence that has preserved a community of thought and agreement about children's book standards, between opposite coasts and wide midlands, sustaining the Medals as a testimony of American children's librarianship.

After the early years of the book awards, the terms of individual chairmen are harder to personalize, because the pattern was set. In the nineteen-forties the weight of office grew heavier and the undertakings more complex. Some of the goals related to the Newbery and Caldecott Awards were: better exchanges of book criticism and opinion between members of the Award Committee; full opportunity for all members to read and know all important books of the year; better publicity for the Medal books at announcement time. Each chairman has given time and effort without measure, in keeping with the very high past order of official performance.

In the matter of writing letters, however, the volume of correspondence that Frederic Melcher's files accumulated, since he stood on the platform at Swampscott and made his impulse known, inspires awe and sympathy. To questions from Award Committee officers he wrote friendly, unhurried, helpful answers, showing the same pleasure in the year's affairs as when the Medals began. The awards reached their maturity under a warm, benevolent sun, in clear air. Never for a moment have they been touched by a special viewpoint or motive, or any shadow of limitation upon their freedom. Frederic Melcher was consulted on technical points, but he remained completely aloof from, and ignorant of, the voting until it was finished. To quote him on a related point, "I have never had from any publisher, any year, any suggestion that I might influence, or know how to influence, the decision." Possibly he bestowed Medals for books he did not like personally, but of this he gave no sign.

These are familiar facts, and have been rightly taken for granted; but here at this time let them be clearly stated for the record.

The chairman in 1940 wrote to the Award Committee, "The procedure is as fair as any could possibly be. Each committee member votes according to her personal conviction, and each vote of course has the same weight. After the balloting commences it is a simple question of majority, and no member knows how another votes. Titles with fewest votes are eliminated in successive rounds, and usually a real consensus of opinion emerges, to give the winning book an ungrudged victory."

Since the 1940s some of the handicaps of distance between members of the Award Committee have been overcome by a planned consultation at the midwinter meeting of the American Library Association. This has proved most valuable, coming at the time of year when discussion can lay the groundwork for agreement much more readily than letters.

No one has sufficiently emphasized the keen edge of professional interest which the Newbery and Caldecott Medals provide for those whose work is connected with children's books. They are a spur to the eternal search for quality, and a boon to the spirit of the children's librarian. Reading and evaluating new hundreds of children's books each year becomes at times a dulling job. The critical faculties slump from overuse. But a day comes when every children's librarian passes judgment, either with a ballot, or perhaps only in her own mind. The incentive to do so, which stems from these Medals, makes them an important, pleasure-giving, vitalizing influence.

Then comes the season of late winter when interest in the award news starts mounting, and ears prick up for every hint of how the winds may blow. After anticipation comes the news itself, and the satisfaction of spreading it, discussing it, expressing opinions. Probably unequaled for excitement was the secrecy formerly surrounding the announcement at the annual conference. Reports spread like wildfire, even the false ones. Nevertheless the audience as a whole, on most occasions, did not know who the recipients would be until they appeared on the platform. That was the moment worth waiting for: the announcement, the surprise that rippled through the auditorium, the applause and the standing ovation. Surely the gift of sheer interest that accrues from the Newbery and Caldecott Medal tradition is deserving of all praise.

The awards were selected as usual during the Second World War years, but no national conferences were held in 1943, 1944, or 1945. The Medals were presented instead at regional conferences in New York and Cleveland and in 1945 at a luncheon in New York given for this special purpose.

An important procedural change on the award calendar was forecast in August 1947, by a letter Frederic Melcher wrote to Virginia Chase, Carnegie Library of Pittsburgh, as the Award Committee Chairman:

There has always been a considerable problem of how to keep the secret until the time of announcement, and this year especially it seemed to leak out. We have tried to keep it by having no one but the chairman of the committee, among the librarians, know what the final result was, the publicity person of A.L.A., and this office, which has to do with getting the winners to the convention. The suggestion has been made that an announcement of the winners might be made in March, immediately on the closing of the ballot, and that the reception and presentation of the medals would take place at the convention as usual.

Those who suggested this felt that there would be the same interest in having the winners as guests, and the same interest in what they said. Actually these speeches are becoming quite an important contribution to our understanding of American children's literature, and the actual presence of the winners should make the occasional memorable.

This is just an idea tossed into the field of discussion, and so I send it on to you. I haven't, of course, talked with any of the publishers about it, and I don't know whether in their experience in publicity the plan would be of advantage or disadvantage.

Miss Chase and her committee were at first reluctant to consider such a change. All declared their fond feelings for the usual surprise announcement at the conference session, before a big audience that waited in suspense.

The question would go before the entire membership at the next conference, but second thoughts of this committee brought forth in the interval some advantages to the proposal. An immediate announcement would add dignity and force to news which was difficult to preserve in secrecy for months. The recurring leaks had frequently softened part of the Medals' impact. Children's book editors talked over the new idea in their Children's Book Council and recommended its good points to Mr. Melcher. Meanwhile C.L.A. officers discussed it, in preparation for the 1948 A.L.A. conference in Atlantic City. There on June 16 at their business meeting the children's librarians voted to adopt this revised plan, beginning in 1949.

"A vital change in procedure for one of the Children's Library Association's most valued undertakings, the announcement of the Newbery-Caldecott awards, was made this June at the Atlantic City Conference when it was recommended and voted upon that an official nationwide announcement of the Newbery-Caldecott awards be made as soon as the voting was completed in March," wrote Margaret M. Clark, chairman-elect, to the membership. "The cherished tradition of the surprise announcement at the annual banquet was carefully weighed against the increasing difficulties of maintaining secrecy through the three or four month period between the completed balloting and the final announcement and awarding of the medals. Other practical reasons for the more immediate announcement were: that it would be more newsworthy at the earlier date, and closer to the period of other scientific and literary awards; that library exhibits and publicity reach a greater number of patrons at that time than in the quieter summer months; and that teachers and parents can immediately cooperate in stimulating interest in the award winners and also the runners-up."

The present calendar for selecting and presenting the awards is as follows:

*November*
Children's Services Division members receive nominating blanks for Medal books.

*December*
Membership nominations are tabulated and sent to Newbery-Caldecott Committee.

*January-February*
Newbery-Caldecott Committee members meet at A.L.A. Midwinter conference to discuss nominated books.
Ballots to conclusion.

*March*
Medals presented to winning author and artist, in New York (on first Monday of month if possible).
Public announcements.
(Medals remain in chairman's possession until next conference of A.L.A.).

*Annual summer conference of American Library Association*
Banquet in honor of award winners and public presentation of engraved medals. Their addresses of acceptance.

Under this recent scheme, which now is in full effect, greater emphasis is placed upon publicizing the awards. Preparations are made in advance for wide news coverage on the March date when the decisions are released. Announcement of the winning books is issued simultaneously from the R. R. Bowker offices in New York and from the Newbery-Caldecott Publicity Committee of the Children's Services Division.

The object is to get the news fully distributed within hours of the announcement. The two major news wires supposedly carry the item to all presses, but newspapers are negligent about printing it. To increase the press coverage, many hundreds of releases are mailed in advance to newspapers and magazines.

The Children's Services Division directs its publicity effort to the local librarian in the average community, who awaits the news so she can display the honored books. The Newbery-Caldecott Publicity Committee (this may be just one person working with the Award Committee chairman) dispatches names of the winners and runners-up to state library agencies, city and state school library supervisors, and heads of public library children's departments in cities of one hundred thousand population and over. This is done in time for news to reach these agencies on the day the announcement is made in New York and Chicago. The real advance indicated by such recent methods depends upon thorough planning and efficiency, and is the work of Children's Services Division officers. The rest of the library profession and interested public receive the

announcement within a few days from *Publishers'
Weekly,* and from the next issues of library and school
journals. The book supplements of leading metropoli-
tan newspapers usually allot some space to the award
news.

The group that witnesses the Medal presentations in
the R. R. Bowker offices is necessarily a small one. The
chairman of the C.S.D. Newbery-Caldecott Committee
comes to New York to conduct the brief ceremony. The
conference banquet is still considered the official occasion, providing the opportunity for the A.L.A. members
to meet the recipients.

The Newbery-Caldecott Committee is now composed
of twenty-three Division members and represents all kinds
of libraries serving boys and girls. It is composed of the
four officers of the Division (president, vice-president,
past president, and treasurer), the Book Evaluation Committee's five members, eight members selected in the annual C.S.D. spring election, and six members appointed
by the C.S.D. president. The vice-president of the Children's Services Division is the chairman of this committee.

In some years, more than twelve votes of first choice,
of a possible twenty-two, give an immediate winner. In
order to win either award, a book must receive twelve
first-choice votes (four points each) for a total of forty-
eight points, *with* a twelve-point lead over the next in
line. Second-choice votes count three points and third-
choice, two points. The number of runners-up is not set,

but is determined each year by the closeness of their totals to the winning total of votes.

Two aspects of this award selecting are considered less than satisfactory, but no solutions are in readiness. One is the problem of availability of the season's new books in smaller communities, where the children's and school librarians are unable to see all possible contenders for the awards. More librarians would send in nominations if they felt fully informed. Furthermore, too few of them have had time to read all the outstanding books, even if they have received them, by December when their ballots are due. The popular vote is thus seriously handicapped by the shortened schedule. Fair-minded members are loath to vote for one favorite title before they have compared any others that might be worth consideration.

The other difficulty is related to the first: that the Committee must vote too soon after the publication of the books, and that more time is needed to prove the value of the season's products and to discover those perhaps less publicized. Children's librarians have raised this point because they want the Newbery and Caldecott Medals to maintain their vital roles and to possess "the imagination to link the past with the present and the future," in the words of Anne Carroll Moore.

As chairman of the Award Committee in 1948, Virginia Chase wrote to her members about matters both timely and recurrent. Her letter characterizes the tone of these undertakings through the years:

No one realizes more clearly than librarians the unevenness of yearly outputs in children's books. Some years are rich while others are meager. . . . When the lean years come we hear the frequent remark, "Why give an award at all? Is it not better to hold it for a good book rather than give it to one that is mediocre?" To omit an award is rather a difficult thing to do. In the first place only one good book out of approximately seven hundred is needed and that is likely to turn up when the sifting begins. . . . There has been in my memory bitter resentment over two choices of the committee and those books have proved to be withstanding the test of time far better than several which were greeted with great fanfare.

And so it goes from year to year with each Committee honestly trying its best to select "the author of the most distinguished contribution to American literature for children" and "the artist of the most distinguished American picture book for children," and each member of the Committee appreciating the honor bestowed upon her to assume this responsibility.

# CHAPTER IX

# The Medal-Winning Books

This narration of events concerning the Newbery and Caldecott Medals comes now to a point where discussion of the books themselves is in order. In keeping with the original purpose, however, of recording the history of the movement, this chapter is more descriptive than critical in its intent. We are interested primarily in what has happened. A thorough evaluation of the award-winning books deserves a separate approach. Reference is therefore again made to the undertaking of *The Horn Book* magazine, to present in two volumes, one for each Medal, a full estimate of the books, as they have been judged by various critics. (See page 69 *n*.) These reviews, together with the acceptance papers of the winning authors and artists, thus receive the ample treatment which is consistent with *The Horn Book*'s function, as a journal of criticism in the field of children's books and reading.

## Books That Have Won the Newbery Medal

Forty-two books have won the Newbery Medal, including *A Wrinkle in Time* by Madeleine L'Engle, published in 1962. (See chronological list, with illustrators and publishers, in Appendix.) Thirty-seven of these are works of fiction. Of the remaining books of subject interest, one is classified as general history, four as biography, in library nonfiction:

| Van Loon | *Story of Mankind* | 1922* |
|----------|--------------------|-------|
| Meigs | *Invincible Louisa* | 1934 |
| Daugherty | *Daniel Boone* | 1940 |
| Yates | *Amos Fortune, Free Man* | 1951 |
| Latham | *"Carry On, Mr. Bowditch"* | 1956 |

Of the thirty-seven fiction titles, nine are fairy tales of various kinds. The majority are single, book-length fantasies:

| Lofting | *The Voyages of Doctor Dolittle* | 1923 |
|---------|----------------------------------|------|
| Coatsworth | *The Cat Who Went to Heaven* | 1931 |
| Lawson | *Rabbit Hill* | 1945 |
| Bailey | *Miss Hickory* | 1947 |
| du Bois | *The Twenty-one Balloons* | 1948 |

The most recent is science fiction:

| L'Engle | *A Wrinkle in Time* | 1963 |
|---------|---------------------|------|

One is legendary history:

| Seredy | *The White Stag* | 1938 |
|--------|------------------|------|

Two are collections of short fairy tales:

| Finger | *Tales from Silver Lands* | 1925 |
|--------|---------------------------|------|
| Chrisman | *Shen of the Sea* | 1926 |

The rest of the Newbery fiction is of a realistic kind. The stories fall into various patterns, according to

---

* Dates used in this enumeration of categories indicate year the awards were presented. Publication was during the year preceding.

schemes used for comparing them, and are remarkable for their range. Eight may be grouped together as American historical fiction. The first three have a very strong appeal for girls and the next three for boys; the central character in each of the final two is a girl.

| Field | *Hitty, Her First Hundred Years* | 1930 |
|---|---|---|
| Brink | *Caddie Woodlawn* | 1936 |
| Sawyer | *Roller Skates* | 1937 |
| Edmonds | *The Matchlock Gun* | 1942 |
| Forbes | *Johnny Tremain* | 1944 |
| Keith | *Rifles for Watie* | 1958 |
| Speare | *The Witch of Blackbird Pond* | 1959 |
| O'Dell | *Island of the Blue Dolphins* | 1961 |

Five Newbery books, of which the first four appeal primarily to girls, are family stories with a modern American background:

| Enright | *Thimble Summer* | 1939 |
|---|---|---|
| Lenski | *Strawberry Girl* | 1946 |
| Estes | *Ginger Pye* | 1952 |
| Sorensen | *Miracles on Maple Hill* | 1957 |
| Krumgold | *Onion John* | 1960 |

Three have English historical settings:

| Hawes | *The Dark Frigate* | 1924 |
|---|---|---|
| Gray | *Adam of the Road* | 1943 |
| deAngeli | *The Door in the Wall* | 1950 |

Three have distinctive geographical settings:

| Mukerji | *Gay Neck* (India) | 1928 |
|---|---|---|
| Kelly | *Trumpeter of Krakow* (Poland) | 1929 |
| DeJong | *Wheel on the School* (Holland) | 1955 |

Next come seven unusual books having in common certain artistic ties. A high quality of writing is one; another, the central consciousness of the boy in each story, which transcends his own experiences, to personify something of his people's destiny. There is engrained nationality in these books. Several depend upon mood, and have slow-moving plots. This is not true of *Young Fu* and *Call It Courage*, in which there is story action of quicker tempo.

| | | |
|---|---|---|
| Armer | *Waterless Mountain* | 1932 |
| Lewis | *Young Fu of the Upper Yangtze* | 1933 |
| Shannon | *Dobry* | 1935 |
| Sperry | *Call It Courage* | 1941 |
| Clark | *Secret of the Andes* | 1953 |
| Krumgold | *And Now Miguel* | 1954 |
| Speare | *The Bronze Bow* | 1962 |

Last item, two horse stories:

| | | |
|---|---|---|
| James | *Smoky, the Cowhorse* | 1927 |
| Henry | *King of the Wind* | 1949 |

That the books honored by award of the Newbery Medal touch the widest twentieth-century dimensions of writing for children has seldom been questioned. Most of them are books of distinction in style and conception, each in turn a genuine "contribution to American literature for children." The one serious, sustained criticism of the books has been on the issue of their popularity.

A variation of this criticism was current in the wake of the nineteen-thirties when much was heard about "the feminization of the awards." That complaint largely replaced the earlier pair, "too old," and "too literary," and it in its turn was quieted by the undeniably masculine writings of James Daugherty, Armstrong Sperry, Walter D. Edmonds, and others who followed. The first eight authors who received the Newbery Medal happened to be men. They spanned the nineteen-twenties. The male run ended with Eric Kelly in 1929, and by curious chance Rachel Field set off a decade of woman medalists, which ended with Elizabeth Enright in 1939. (Since then there have been no such neat regularities to attract the historian, unless the late 1950s and early 1960s be associated with a trend toward the American background.) There was indeed a scarcity of first-class authors writing for boys in the nineteen-thirties, but out of those years came many books which were not limited either to boy or girl readers and still command the respect of a good audience.

Three Newbery books that stand out for their real satisfaction to a majority of children are *Ginger Pye, King of the Wind,* and *The Witch of Blackbird Pond.* Eleanor Estes' *Ginger Pye,* written in the delectable vein of her *Moffats* stories, tells of the engaging Pye family and their dog Ginger, in monumental everyday affairs with which the younger Pyes are earnestly occupied. *King of the Wind* by Marguerite Henry has all the thunder of a full-blooded horse story, which assures its favor with a large section of enthusiastic fans. An eighteenth-century setting seems no handicap to popularity, with Godolphin Arabian in the foreground. He was the great stallion sent by the Sultan of Morocco to young Louis XV of France. New England discipline, humanity, and love illuminate Elizabeth George Speare's *The Witch of Blackbird Pond,* a thoughtful yet exciting story of a seventeenth-century Puritan community.

Five other Newbery Medal books usually found in the upper bracket of favor among children are *Johnny Tremain, Rabbit Hill, Voyages of Doctor Dolittle, Caddie Woodlawn,* and *Strawberry Girl.* A possible sixth is *A Wrinkle in Time* by Madeleine L'Engle, which has received a mixed reaction, thus far, but in some libraries is decidedly popular. It is a complex fantasy involving other planets, and the evil that hovers among them. Older boys and girls welcomed on publication *Johnny Tremain* by Esther Forbes, and the continuing demand is a credit to their taste. The silversmith's apprentice who early in the Revolution joined the patriots' cause as messenger boy is a believable hero whose character and services were worthy of the times.

*Rabbit Hill* by Robert Lawson, and the three other books last mentioned, are enjoyed by children in the middle age group. Lawson's perceptive knowledge of the little animals in his garden, dependent upon the householders for planting and sharing a crop of vegetables, inspired this masterpiece of humor and fancy. Hugh Lofting's *Voyages of Doctor Dolittle* is related in theme, although quite unhampered by natural science, being about the kindness and linguistic genius of the good doctor who understood animals' talk and traveled far and wide to cure their ills. It is twenty-two years older than Lawson's book, but age in a well-loved story means nothing to children. Both these gentle wildlife whimsies make very good reading aloud.

The remaining two books are preferred by girls who, like the heroines of *Caddie Woodlawn* and *Strawberry Girl,* are about ten years old. *Caddie Woodlawn* by Carol

Ryrie Brink is a lively family tale of the Wisconsin frontier in the sixties. *Strawberry Girl* by Lois Lenski describes a little-known way of life on a backwoods farm in Florida. Both authors know their locales, and their stories meet the test of time on solid foundations.

We come now to twenty Newbery books which occupy the middle ground between actual popularity and a prevailing lack of it. Four are well-known stories for older boys: *Call It Courage, The Matchlock Gun, Rifles for Watie,* and *Smoky, the Cowhorse. Call It Courage* by Armstrong Sperry has often been called a miniature masterpiece. In its terse pages a timid Polynesian boy faces testing experiences, and alone and unaided, conquers his fear. *The Matchlock Gun* by Walter D. Edmonds is a drama which gives no pause for questions, in the terrifying hour of an Indian attack. This is a true, stirring episode from New York State's early history. *Rifles for Watie* by Harold Keith is a long junior novel based on journals of Civil War soldiers. The lesser-known campaigns in Oklahoma and Kansas have intense reality in this story of army hardship and fatigue. *Smoky, the Cowhorse* is the famous, lifelike yarn from the cattle country by Will James. Now thirty years old, it still maintains a medium popularity. Publicity and book talks can create an interest in a book during its first season, but in afterseasons not much is done to bolster its status. The longevity of many of these award books deserves emphatic notice. Disregarding their age we are considering only their present demand, after wide acclaim in many cases has long since passed. They have occupied their regular place in the library collection for years, without the help of fanfare. Perhaps *The Bronze Bow* by Elizabeth George Speare will prove fully as durable. Its fine characterizations and vivid background portray the time of Jesus and the early Christians.

Six stories for girls which maintain a quiet average of library use are: *Island of the Blue Dolphins, Miss Hickory, Hitty, Roller Skates, Thimble Summer,* and *Miracles on Maple Hill. Island of the Blue Dolphins* by Scott O'Dell is a feminine Crusoe tale of an Indian girl, alone on an island near California, over a century ago. When the right readers find this book, its special quality is appreciated. *Miss Hickory* by Carolyn Sherwin Bailey is the spicy chronicle of a doll made of applewood, with a hickory-nut head, who weathers a New Hampshire winter outdoors. It is flavored with New England to the last shred of Miss Hickory's dignity. Also a doll story, and of great renown, is Rachel Field's *Hitty,* an even sturdier piece of New England, carved in Maine from mountain ashwood. Hitty had lived through a hundred years of journeys, adventures, and vast change when her biography was retraced by a gifted storyteller. *Roller Skates* by Ruth Sawyer finds many appreciative girls to share the joys of ten-year-old Lucinda whose sparkling year of freedom was lived to the brim in New York, back in the nineties. *Thimble Summer* by Elizabeth Enright recalls the happy, contented season spent by a very real little girl on a modern Wisconsin farm. Kindness of spirit, between people and toward animals, glows in *Miracles on Maple Hill* by Virginia Sorensen. For a city child and her family, this Pennsylvania farm community abounds in the miracles of nature. These six stories are warm and wise in human relationships. Their authors have fine values, woven together for their readers in terms of real life; girls especially, between nine and eleven years of age, understand what is offered here.

Reaction to Marguerite deAngeli's *The Door in the Wall* varies somewhat in the libraries consulted. In some localities it is popular with both boys and girls, while other groups are only mildly interested in Robin's story, set in a medieval English monastery and castle at the time of the London plague. *Young Fu of the Upper Yangtze* by Elizabeth Foreman Lewis falls in a mixed category also. The picture it records of China in the early nineteen-thirties deserves recognition for its historical value, but the generation that Young Fu typified has lost some of its contact with Western readers of a later generation. *Wheel on the School* by Meindert DeJong is a simple story about a small Dutch village, where the children make their school roof an inviting·place for storks to nest. Sincere in tone and slow in action, this has not won general popularity but it finds readers, both boys and girls.

A modern long fairy tale and an older collection of short fairy tales seem to attract less than average use, *The Twenty-one Balloons* and *Tales from Silver Lands*. William Pène du Bois concocted a clever mixture of science and fiction when he wrote *The Twenty-one Balloons*. The fantastic adventures of Professor Sherman in his marvelous 1883 balloon are as amusing to grownups as to children. Charles Finger's *Tales from Silver Lands* is a collection of nineteen legends which the author heard in South America and retold with drama and flavor, providing material often used by storytellers.

The four Newbery biographies and Hendrik Van Loon's *Story of Mankind* enjoy a fair and steady popularity, the latter to a lesser degree than the biographies. Van Loon's spirited history is used a great deal in the children's rooms to answer reference questions, but is not so much read as a book. The biographies also meet specific needs for subject material, but each is read in its own right to a well-deserved and gratifying degree. The oldest, *Invincible Louisa* by Cornelia Meigs is an intimate study of Louisa May Alcott, her family, and their distinguished friends in Concord. The great pioneer *Daniel Boone* is the subject of James Daugherty's stirring prose and pictures, which together do justice to Boone's courage and human qualities. In *Amos Fortune, Free Man* Elizabeth Yates tells the poignant story of a Negro who rose from slavery to honored citizenship, through dignity that triumphed over degradation. This testament spans a long lifetime, from 1710 to 1801. *"Carry On, Mr. Bowditch,"* by Jean L. Latham is a fictionized biography of Nathaniel Bowditch, the navigation expert. Some libraries class this as fiction, for despite all its interest in mathematics, it reads like a sea story. The best appreciation of it comes from boys who have acquired some scientific background.

A dozen Newbery Medal books compose a group considered lowest in popularity. Five of these are more or less historic and distant in setting, from the seventeenth-century English sea story *The Dark Frigate* by Charles Boardman Hawes to *Gay Neck* by Dhan Gopal Mukerji, which tells of the beautiful Calcutta-born carrier pigeon that served as a messenger in World War I. *Adam of the*

*Road* by Elizabeth Janet Gray is the thirteenth-century adventure story of an English boy searching the King's Highway for his father, and is told against a lively background of minstrel art. *Dobry* by Monica Shannon describes in vivid terms what peasant life in middle Europe was, some years ago; Dobry, a Bulgarian boy, longs to become a sculptor. *Trumpeter of Krakow* by Eric P. Kelly takes the reader back to fifteenth-century Poland, in a masterpiece based upon Polish tradition. Its tangled, exciting mysteries surround a precious national jewel, and involve a patriotic boy trumpeter stationed in a Krakow church tower. Far removed in time and space is *Onion John* by Joseph Krumgold, a modern American story of a wise and humble immigrant, whose fervent friend is a young boy.

Three fairy tales of unlike character fall into this category of comparative neglect today: *The White Stag, The Cat Who Went to Heaven,* and, to a lesser degree, *Shen of the Sea.* The inspired prose and drawings of Kate Seredy in her epic *The White Stag* come from the legendary past of the Hungarian people, telling of the migration from Asia of ancient Huns and Magyars, led by the feared Attila. Elizabeth Coatsworth's *The Cat Who Went to Heaven* is a gently spiritual fairy tale about a Japanese artist, his little cat Good Fortune, and the miracle wrought by Buddha. It has had, and still maintains, appeal for imaginative children who respond to its special quality. Arthur Bowie Chrisman gives a genuine atmosphere of old China to his *Shen of the Sea,* a collection of sixteen short, bright fairy tales which have amused many a story-hour audience.

We conclude the roll of Newbery Medal winners with three movingly written books, each a product of fine craftsmanship and sensitivity. *Secret of the Andes, And Now Miguel,* and *Waterless Mountain* are books of more atmosphere and less direct story than appeal to average library readers. They are books for children of particular taste.

*Secret of the Andes* by Ann Nolan Clark is unforgettably staged in a high Peruvian valley, where an Inca shepherd boy guards a herd of llamas and also a sacred trust for his ancient people. *And Now Miguel* is Joseph Krumgold's beautiful prose portrait of New Mexican herdsmen, and of the boy Miguel, who is portrayed with rare understanding. *Waterless Mountain* by Laura Adams Armer has never found readers in good number to appreciate its story of a Navajo boy being prepared for his duties as a medicine man. The quiet subtleties of imagination and mysticism in these three artistic stories apparently fail to arrest the interest of most fast-moving young Americans in a noisy age. However there are those prized readers who do respond to such writing, and for these the children's librarian is proud of her means to make these satisfying recommendations.

Many voices of distress have been raised after it has been found that a Newbery book is regarded without enthusiasm by majorities of children's room readers. In all probability that issue will reassert itself many times. On the question of the Medal books' popularity with children, Louise Seaman Bechtel once wrote to Frederic Melcher, "I am beginning to feel that *that,* as an immediate qualification, is not so necessary. The Medals should hold up standards on writing and art—and if they are above a current average, so much the better!"

The danger of awards which are *not* "above a current average" should cause at least equal concern. The whole tendency today being to popularize and standardize, perhaps children's book standards must inevitably feel the same creeping influence. But so far as the Newbery and Caldecott Medals are concerned, those standards are in the sole hands of librarians involved with children's books, who can afford to rebuff the advances of mediocrity. Children's librarians are duly anxious for the honored books to be liked by children. This is healthy within reason, but standards are at stake which mean life or death to the Medals. The ideal they represent is a lofty one which smothers close to the ground, and breathes its proper air head and shoulders above the crowd. Today when children's books must first be appraised in the commodity market, the noncommercial purity of these awards is refreshing to contemplate.

As in most American-made products, various national origins soon were represented on the Newbery honor roll, as sons of Holland, England, and India won early places. Ireland and Hungary gave daughters in the next few years. All of course were living in the United States more or less permanently when this recognition was accorded them. The 1955 winner, Meindert DeJong, was, like Hendrik Van Loon, born in Holland.

Caldecott Medal books display even more variety with respect to national influences. This variety has long been the unique claim of picture books in America, where artists from every country have found appreciation. To compare the diversified backgrounds of the artists on the Caldecott honor roll is to discover the cosmopolitan confluence of talent at work in the field of modern picture book art.

The younger Caldecott Medal seems on the whole to arouse less contention than its companion award. Children's librarians, for one reason, feel on their own solid ground as judges of literature, while being perhaps timid about art criticism, in which fewer are experts. Besides, picture books as a class are naturally popular.

Men and women artists have shared Caldecott honors almost equally. Three famous husband-and-wife teams have won this Medal: the d'Aulaires, the Petershams, and the Haders. A man and a woman, Robert McCloskey and Marcia Brown, have each received the Medal twice. Thus far Robert Lawson has been the only winner of both Newbery and Caldecott Medals.

### Books That Have Won the Caldecott Medal

Twenty-six books have won the Caldecott Medal, including *The Snowy Day* by Ezra Jack Keats, published in 1962. (See list in Appendix.)

In the library children's rooms the picture books are those books of which there are rarely enough, from whose corner glows the irresistible attraction of color and animation. Their eye-catching pages, with brief, easily read texts, provide entertainment for all but the most invulnerable human beings, regardless of age. Questions of picture-book popularity are largely academic.

The Caldecott Medal books are easier to place in a popular rating than the Newbery books, for reaction to them is less complicated, and, over the years, more consistent.

The two top favorites with children seem to be:

| Ward | *The Biggest Bear* | 1953 |
| Bemelmans | *Madeline's Rescue* | 1954 |

These books possess the qualities for both immediate and enduring appeal. *The Biggest Bear,* written by Lynd Ward and illustrated with his bold yet softened black and white drawings, is an impressive book. Men, trees, and bear tower in the pictures. There is overawing bigness in every page, which shrinks the size (and influence) of the little boy. The artist tells his exciting story in a particularly exciting medium.

*Madeline's Rescue* by Ludwig Bemelmans combines the virtues suggested by the words "picture book" but seldom provided with real generosity in one package. It is big, colorful, humorous; has real story; is crammed with pictures, upon which hang the interest and suspense. Those who may not know the changeless popularity of the predecessor, *Madeline,* might judge at first glance that these pictures are too sophisticated for small children's choice. The truth is, however, that they could not please the audience better. They are joyously racy, yet simple at heart and easy to understand.

Those deemed next in the popular regard are:

| d'Aulaire | *Abraham Lincoln* | 1940 |
| McCloskey | *Make Way for Ducklings* | 1942 |

| Mordvinoff | *Finders Keepers* | 1952 |
| Brown | *Cinderella* | 1955 |
| Rojankovsky | *Frog Went a-Courtin'* | 1956 |
| Brown | *Once A Mouse . . .* | 1962 |
| Keats | *The Snowy Day* | 1963 |

The two older ones are fine big books with appeal on every page for successive audiences who continually arrive at the age and place to enjoy them. The eight-year-olds may discover the d'Aulaire picture book, but younger children are entertained by most of those listed here. The earnest depth of text and pictures in *Abraham Lincoln* by Ingri and Edgar d'Aulaire has meaning for every reader. Bright lithographs in the colors of homespun express the full significance of this short but balanced story-biography. Robert McCloskey's *Make Way for Ducklings* tells an amusing, kindly incident about the Mallard family's eight ducklings in Boston traffic, serenely crossing to the Public Garden. The warm sepia drawings do justice to the sympathy of Bostonians, and to their famous midtown scenery. The problems of two dogs with one bone are solved in exuberant colors by Nicolas Mordvinoff in *Finders Keepers,* by "Will and Nicolas." The striking modern reds and yellows, and black with ginger, accent a different note in Caldecott Medal art. Its adult admirers increase as the book's popularity with children stands proven. Marcia Brown's beautiful illustrations of *Cinderella* have fine fairy-tale quality. The old magic favorite from Perrault remains dear to young hearts —far more so when freshly interpreted by the right artist. Her three-color woodcuts in *Once A Mouse . . .* dramatize the Indian fable of a mouse's unsuccessful transformation. Several sources can take credit for a familiar Scottish ballad coming out in picture-book array, *Frog Went A-Courtin'*. John Langstaff arranged the text, and the prize-winning illustrations are by Feodor Rojankovsky. The gay bustling in these colorful pages, occasioned by the wedding feast of Frog and Miss Mousie, pleases the eye, just as the verses have tickled many an ear.

Although it is the latest winner, Ezra Jack Keats' *The Snowy Day* seems to have made its place immediately in this group. Pre-school children enter into its happy, child-like reflections and understand the mood of its water colors.

Now we come to a middle group of picture books which year after year hold to their average popularity. They are loved by many children, and are also helped in finding larger audiences when the librarians give them personal introductions.

| | | |
|---|---|---|
| Handforth | *Mei Li* | 1939 |
| Burton | *The Little House* | 1943 |
| Slobodkin | *Many Moons* | 1944 |
| Jones | *Prayer for a Child* | 1945 |
| Petersham | *The Rooster Crows* | 1946 |
| Duvoisin | *White Snow, Bright Snow* | 1948 |
| Hader | *The Big Snow* | 1949 |
| Simont | *A Tree Is Nice* | 1957 |
| McCloskey | *Time of Wonder* | 1958 |
| Ets | *Nine Days to Christmas* | 1960 |

Most of these contain a familiar hominess of theme and simple realism in pictures which small children immediately understand. *The Little House,* written and illustrated by Virginia Lee Burton, is a quiet book that gets along without people until the very end. Its pages are varied and delightful in their fresh, pleasant colors. The pathetically deserted house, isolated in the city, appeals to children's sympathies. No little house has more friends. It is easy to associate with it Janice May Udry's *A Tree Is Nice.* In harmony with the many kinds of beautiful trees pictured by Marc Simont, this is a tall book. Perhaps less popular is *Prayer for a Child,* written by Rachel Field, with Elizabeth Orton Jones' illustrations in soft pastel colors expressing the faith of childhood. Parents and teachers are grateful borrowers of this small book, and also of *The Rooster Crows,* the collection of American rhymes and jingles which Maud and Miska Petersham set to color. Their clear gay pictures state the character of this book, one of liveliness and strength. Berta and Elmer Hader's *The Big Snow* has lovely still scenes, safe for the scurry of little animals as they seek food and protection near the artists' house after the big snow. The Haders reveal in these pages their long experience as illustrators, and their knowledge of small wildlife that is a steady influence in their work.

The climate of *White Snow, Bright Snow,* written by Alvin Tresselt, is similar, but Roger Duvoisin's pictures are bolder and flatter in design. They also describe beautifully, in their different way, the deep white magic of a snow-covered world, with bright colors bringing some activity into another quiet kind of book. On the Maine coast gentle weather changes to screaming wind in the luminous water colors of Robert McCloskey's large picture book, *Time of Wonder.* Seaside colors in a drama of weather fill these pages with beauty for many receptive children.

A fable and a Chinese incident complete the picture-book group which has in common this fair degree of popularity. *Many Moons,* written by James Thurber in his own well-seasoned style, is a philosophical bit about the whim of a princess that confounds the wise men and is solved by the court fool. Scintillating pictures by Louis Slobodkin are modern-styled and well matched to Thurber's humor. These pictures rely upon suggestion more than graphic detail to tell their story. Their bright hues are a special attraction, enjoyed by children up to nine and ten. The big-sized picture books have a kind of authority, and Thomas Handforth's *Mei Li* possesses proper dimensions for the forceful vitality in its distinguished art work. These black and white drawings are picturesque, with a childlike dignity. They take the reader to the Peking Fair with Mei Li, a little girl of China who goes there and sees the sights. Interest in this book is enduring and its value increases. Closer to our here and now is the story by Marie Hall Ets and Aurora Labastida about little Ceci's anticipations of a wonderful Mexican Christmas. *Nine Days to Christmas* has seasonal popularity. Its soft colors on gray background are unique in their effect.

The final group of Caldecott Medal books, happily not a large one, consists of those which are not often sought by children themselves:

| | | |
|---|---|---|
| Lathrop | *Animals of the Bible* | 1938 |
| Lawson | *They Were Strong and Good* | 1941 |
| Weisgard | *The Little Island* | 1947 |

| Politi | *Song of the Swallows* | 1950 |
| Milhous | *The Egg Tree* | 1951 |
| Cooney | *Chanticleer and the Fox* | 1959 |
| Sidjakov | *Baboushka and the Three Kings* | 1961 |

Three of these enjoy periodic favor and are requested by parents and teachers. Around Easter time adults and children are very eager for copies of *The Egg Tree* by Katharine Milhous, which is of course a story about a small tree hung with colored Easter eggs. The pictures' soft bright colors in Pennsylvania Dutch style reflect the origin of the custom. Dorothy Lathrop's *Animals of the Bible,* the first book to receive the Caldecott Medal, illustrates Bible passages which have to do with animals, as chosen by Helen Dean Fish. There is fine Biblical feeling in the pages, drawn with the artist's special knowledge of animal life, in black and white. *Baboushka and the Three Kings* by Ruth Robbins, illustrated by Nicolas Sidjakov, is a small, richly colored book, adapted from a Russian folk tale with a Christmas theme. This is an artist's book, wonderful in typography, which needs introducing to young children.

The four left seem to be the least popular in average libraries, although *The Little Island* by Golden MacDonald, illustrated by Leonard Weisgard, does appeal to many children. Its soft blues, greens, and browns are faithful to nature's cycles, for this story records the seasons and life patterns on a small lonely island. *Chanticleer and the Fox* by Barbara Cooney also finds genuine appreciation, but not every child grasps it. The clear colors bring sparkling life to the medieval scenes, in a robust adaptation from one of Chaucer's *Canterbury*

*Tales.* There is great stillness in *Song of the Swallows* by Leo Politi, and calm, motionless color, to reflect the joy of the old gardener and small boy at San Juan Capistrano Mission when the swallows return. *They Were Strong and Good* by Robert Lawson contains some of the most moving pages in all our picture books—the scene, for example, which shows the boy soldier limping home from the Civil War. Children about nine to eleven are the most likely readers of this story, which places it beyond the popularity age for picture books. Lawson offers a chronicle, with the help of distinguished drawings, of his own forebears. They, like most Americans, "were not great or famous, but they were strong and good. They worked hard and had many children."

To sum up, four of the Caldecott Medal books are illustrated in black and white, one in sepia, twenty-one in two or more colors. There is little resemblance among the styles of the artists represented here, so no critic on viewing the display can accuse our most acclaimed picture books, representing the last twenty years, of domination by any art school. They are, it is clear, in a healthy state of free-wheeling readiness to travel in all directions.

There was a period of uncertain outlook for picture books soon after the Caldecott Medal was established. They ran into bad times during and after World War II, when shortages of material and rising labor costs drove the price of color printing up into a high luxury bracket. The beautiful productions in several colors of the nineteen-thirties became wonders of a cherished past. Artists found themselves seriously hampered by the new facts, and untried economies in method had to be devised.

An up-to-date display of Caldecott Medal books proves that talent and ingenuity triumphed. The publishers deserve major credit for each conquest, won by trial and error, and refusal to let costs drain out all color from bookmaking.

Any uneasiness about "trends" in both awards has gradually dissolved, as the pool of honored books widens, year by year. Their sheer diversity finally proved to their gloomiest critics the one rigid fact that as to type they are completely unpredictable. Children's librarians have reached the practical philosophy that whether or not they agree on a selection, the exercise of choosing is important, and the yearly focus its own best advocate.

Some reflections by Frederic Melcher in 1946 wisely summarized what had been accomplished: "Masterpieces are not created on order, but warm and thoughtful appreciation, coming promptly after the books are issued, means much to the creative artist. The winners of these Medals find tens of thousands of new readers. The honor is printed to their credit for years to come. Every new book of theirs has the better chance for a hearing. A great and growing audience does not guarantee that we shall have great books, but the expectancy that such an audience creates cannot but give confidence that in the continuance of the upward curve in the quality and beauty of our books for children, the promise of the past twenty-five years of experience with these awards will be fulfilled."

# CHAPTER X

## Influences of the Medals

Children's librarians do not object to being classed as idealists. They mean for children to have the best, and they want to believe that children prefer it. "Choose the best and soon habit will make you prefer it" is an axiom trusted and used by the profession whose fundamental concern is the literary welfare of the young. Children's librarians are simply keeping faith with their own principles when they pay tribute to books of outstanding quality, acknowledging at the same time that these books may appeal to a limited number of readers. There is for them the always heartening factor of the individual child's appreciation, which continually confirms all children's instinct for truth, encountered in books or elsewhere.

It would be gratifying to prove step by step that our two Medals have improved children's books. We believe this to be so, but their weight abides in the attitude they have built. Their influence is a generality, and there is no concrete way to pinpoint causes and effects. The award books show what can be done. They provide a regularly renewed, firm, accessible guide for measuring literary and artistic endeavor. Most of them are very good examples, in theory of course our best examples, of standards the critics uphold. They are ideals demonstrated.

The effect of the Newbery and Caldecott Medals upon writing, illustration, book criticism, children's reading, and children's literature has been indicated or implied in each step of this history. An attempt to retrace the pattern in further detail would require unnecessary restatement of the entire theme. The object of this chapter therefore will be to bring together the opinions of a few other judges who have given thought to the Medals' accomplishments over the years.

One with a long memory and indisputable knowledge was Boston's Alice Jordan, pioneer children's librarian, book critic, and historian. Miss Jordan said in a letter dated February 28, 1954:

I remember so well that meeting in the big drafty building on the New Ocean House grounds in Swampscott, in 1921. How thrilled we all were by Mr. Melcher's announcement, and how enthusiastically all the children's librarians responded to the lift in spirit that his generous offer brought!

In the thirty years that have passed since then it has certainly been clear that one of the influential factors contributing to the remarkable improvement in the making of children's books in America, has been the Newbery Award. Frederic Melcher's vision, so sincerely and tangibly supported, has brought a deeper recognition, more widely felt, of the essence of quality in the writing and publishing of children's books.

"Just the existence of such an award," said Frederic Melcher,

has given children's books a place beside other literature in the minds of authors and the public; the responsibility for the award leads librarians to give more careful study to the new books; as the years go by librarians will come to have more knowledge of the problems of writing and publishing and to have influence on both; the fresh interest in the evaluating of new books gave stimulus to the historical development of children's books; the recurring appearance of John Newbery's name increased this interest. The award has added to the useful activities of the Children's Library Association; it has a useful place through the annual banquets to the winners, at A.L.A. conventions.

There are children's book awards in the United States which take, primarily, the children's viewpoint into consideration. The Newbery-Caldecott Medals set standards rather than catering to them; therefore improvements in content and design can be fairly placed in their direct line of influence.

Julia Sauer of the Rochester (New York) Public Library once made a telling summation of the way in which book prizes are involved with popular taste. Without mentioning Newbery and Caldecott Medals, she contributes in this statement to the understanding of their true principle:

Lately there has been much emphasis on children's reaction to children's books. Awards are being made on the basis of a book's popularity with children. Obviously it would be absurd to say that any children's book is a good children's book if no child reads it. But it is equally absurd to say that the best children's books are necessarily those which are most popular with the children. A child's enthusiasm for a particular title does not give it literary distinction. If that were true we might as well make our awards to the comics and call it a day. Such polls are valuable in showing children's needs and tastes and current trends. But they should not be allowed to set standards, nor should they be confused with standards. It is an exciting experience to find a class voting for something that we know is good; it is rewarding to watch improvement in taste and judgment, but a child's opinion should not be misconstrued by those who make or by those who buy books. It is not a final test. (*The Horn Book* magazine, September-October 1949)

In evaluating this modern enterprise that we call, sometimes fulsomely, children's literature, librarians must make their decisions conscientiously, then be willing to defend them if necessary. Critical tastes for the creative arts do not and need not agree, and a book may quite fairly arouse controversy. But the struggle is healthy, all the more so according to the number of books in competition. Besides those that win highest honors, the runners-up and all the aspirants continually enrich the modern book collection.

Here are the words of Bertha Mahony Miller of *The Horn Book* magazine, summing up for the Medals in the *Friendly Reminiscences* volume made for Frederic Melcher in 1945:

As we watched and applauded the giving of that first Award to Hendrik Van Loon's *Story of Mankind,* we did not dream how strong the brightening influence of this award was to be upon authors and illustrators, publishers, children's librarians, and the bookbuying public. Having watched its effect now for twenty-three years, I believe its first value has been the building of critical judgment. The part criticism plays in any branch of art does not seem to be understood. No art comes to fulfillment without sound criticism, which is just as much able analysis of a book's good points as its weak ones. Criticism also means the growth of a point of view, or a measuring stick, through plentiful reading of the best. It is of prime importance that the Newbery and Caldecott medals are helping to develop critics. . . . Since they are critical awards [they] have had an incalculably stimulating effect not only upon authors, artists, and publishers, but also upon the public interest in children's books. Since the medals are given in the early summer, they have helped to sustain book interest throughout the year and have pointed up Book Week. . . . Children's books have finally come to take their place in the thoughtful American mind as an important part of general literature and art. They are published throughout the year, and sold the year around. In bringing this about Frederic Melcher has had a large part.

Finally, "The importance of your book rests, it seems to me, on the absolute sincerity and conviction of Frederic Melcher that children's books are important," said Anne Carroll Moore, apropos of this volume.

There we gladly rest the case.

# CHAPTER XI

## *The King's Breakfast*

The scene revolving each year has brought around many presentations of awards since the first Newbery Medal author received his applause, and since a Caldecott artist took his place on the platform for a sharing of honors. With these years have come high moments and the enrichment of custom. The human history of the Medals deepens steadily, being renewed and freshened by the personalities and uncommon talents it adds on and on to the record. Satisfaction and stimulus from the occasions are the librarians' reward. However, the winners too may have taken away with their bronze Medals some memories— of a warm-hearted audience, giving to those whom it honored the rare gift of appreciation.

Children's librarians as an audience have few equals for making their guests happy, grateful, and inspired. Some of this group magic has been known to rub off on chance spectators, who had not encountered the lures of the children's book realm until they attended an award celebration. Perhaps children's librarians absorb from the tides of life in their children's rooms, day after day, their communicable good humor and sympathy. This they give back freely to the authors and artists who have put their best into children's books. Whatever the sources, there are currents of understanding between audience and platform. May these be cherished and bequeathed to new children's librarians and their many allies, for the welfare of all who perpetuate a literature for the young. The power of the spirit has not been routed from these strongholds.

Daniel Melcher, President of the R. R. Bowker Company, will continue to provide these Medals through the A.L.A. in memory of his father. Frederic Melcher gave continuity of meaning to award occasions. He delighted in the myriad pieces of his own kaleidoscopic recollections. For the presentation of the first Newbery Medal he traveled overnight to Detroit with Hendrik Van Loon. When they arrived a band was playing on the station platform. For a moment it looked to Mr. Melcher as if the American Library Association were "taking this thing seriously," but just then the cartoonist George McManus stepped off the train and was escorted away by the band, leaving the two bookmen with their chuckles and dignity.

Laura Adams Armer wrote Mr. Melcher that after her *Waterless Mountain* was announced as the winner of the 1932 Medal, she received this note, sent with a basket of flowers, from Mr. Van Loon:

A flower for you Madam and thank you for not having written your book ten years earlier, for then I would not have been able as I am now, to offer you the sincere congratulations of the first recipient of the Newbery Medal, and the Humble Duties of your very obedient servant,

Hendrik Van Loon

Fragments of memories can be chosen at random from

the varied human document. At the 1923 conference, after Hugh Lofting had accepted the second Newbery Medal, Mr. R. R. Bowker asked him how Doctor Dolittle originated. Lofting said that at the front during the First World War he had been so impressed by the behavior of horses and mules under fire that he invented the little doctor to do for them what was not and could not be done in real life. . . . A deeply moved audience rose to its feet as Mrs. Charles Boardman Hawes, widowed a few months before, accepted the 1924 Newbery Medal for Mr. Hawes, who had died at the age of thirty-four. . . . Charles Finger accepted his Medal for 1925 in an outdoor ceremony at the University of Washington in Seattle, under tall campus shade trees. . . . The next year Victorian England was present in authentic person at Atlantic City, when courtly, side-whiskered Fenton Newbery was a guest of honor. . . . Another year Dhan Gopal Mukerji was hidden away among the trees on the French Lick (Indiana) hotel grounds, to avoid discovery before the proper time. . . . When Eric Kelly was given his Medal a Marine Corps bugler sent thrills up every spine by playing the "Heynal," traditional Polish theme, on the original trumpet used for hundreds of years by trumpeters of Krakow. This historic treasure had been loaned to Kelly by the Krakow City Councillors, in tribute to his story.

Since the big Newbery-Caldecott dinners began adding evening glamour to Award Day, they have provided fresh sequences of Medal history, complete with footlights and flower-decked tables. Conference cities across the nation reflect in the pool of remembered ceremonies their own gala auditorium or hotel ballroom scenes.

Worth such preservation were the bright hues of Chinese tapestries and lanterns, and Mr. Melcher dressed as an Oriental sage to match the decor, for Thomas Handforth's *Mei Li* in San Francisco. . . .

Then in Cincinnati a whisper was rampant that the honor guests were "locked up," so closely were the d'Aulaires and James Daugherty guarded in their hotel rooms until their presence could be revealed. For the banquet that evening an ice cream replica had been created of Toby Tyler, Frederic Melcher's favorite character in children's books. ("Mr. Melcher no doubt remembers vividly how he had to ad lib for almost an hour before the singers arrived," wrote Lesley Newton from the Lakewood, Ohio, Public Library, who was chairman that year. "No one else could have done it with so much aplomb.") . . .

A glowing memory from Boston: Anne Carroll Moore and Alice Jordan receiving silver loving cups from their Section, on the stage above the Symphony Hall orchestra pit, just before a Pops Concert entertained the dinner guests. That hot June afternoon in Harvard Yard the Medals had been presented to Armstrong Sperry and Robert Lawson, standing before Harvard's crimson velvet curtain in the Commencement Tent. Sperry was addressing a throng of two thousand or more when a violent storm struck Cambridge. The crowd pushed inward to dry positions, trying to escape the downstreams from the canopy overhead, which sagged with rain water. Sperry, unyielding against the flood, chanted Polynesian songs to the thunder's roar. . . .

Other delightful recollections were of five hundred

people trying to hear Roger Duvoisin by trans-Atlantic telephone from Paris, and of troubadours serenading Ann Nolan Clark with haunting Peruvian folksongs . . . And there were many others . . .

The children's editors who have published the Newbery and Caldecott Medal books of the year generously share the arrangements for conference festivity. Their ingenious devices frequently ornament the award occasions, as expressions of their regard for Frederic Melcher, as well as their partnership with librarians in annual convention.

Until his death the feature role of toastmaster at the dinners belonged of course to Frederic Melcher. In his accustomed place he bound the scenes together, gave them background and sentiment. Often he had to improvise, tell stories, fill in, to save the situation when the program timing failed. "A man of infinite resource and sagacity," James Daugherty once quoted in comment.

The scenes revolve, but they lead with one accord to a certain highlight when, by popular demand, the donor of the Medals read "The King's Breakfast"!

Frederic Melcher, bookman, was a connoisseur of poetry, and rarely happier than when reading it aloud, which he did with skill and effect. His audience might be a neighborly group around a fireplace, or a school assembly in Montclair, New Jersey (where he was long a member of the Board of Education), or thousands in a banquet hall. Robert Frost, Vachel Lindsay, and Carl Sandburg held poetic priorities in his affections, but there remained a well-polished niche in his inner circle of favorites, reserved for A. A. Milne. In Japan in 1947 Milne's verses acquired new meaning for Mr. Melcher, through the wartime experiences of the Tokyo family he was visiting. These friends described destruction in their city by incendiary bombs. On the night when their own home burned they had taken one book with them into the dugout. Their library of ten thousand volumes was lost in the flames, every book except that one—the English edition of *When We Were Very Young*. Mr. Melcher tells this story in a recording made for the Children's Book Council, then reads "The King's Breakfast" by Milne, just as he regularly did at the Award dinners afterwards, despite his protests against honoring the precedent.

A handsome metal plaque was presented to Frederic Melcher by the children's librarians celebrating their fiftieth year of organization in Cleveland at the 1950 American Library Association conference. The inscription thanks Mr. Melcher "for his distinguished contribution to the advancement and encouragement of outstanding literature and art in children's books." The plaque stood on a bookshelf in his office, facing his desk.

He treasured a large, leather-bound scrapbook, presented in 1945 by the children's editors, to mark his fiftieth anniversary in the book business. Its contents are letters to him, one from each editor, and one from every Newbery and Caldecott Medal winner, up to 1945, who was then living. The pages in this handsome anthology speak individually, in the words and drawings of men and women who shaped children's literature, to an eminent degree, for three decades and more. Every page invites quotation, as a few choices will show.

Elizabeth Janet Gray wrote:

I would like to remind you of an occasion which you have perhaps forgotten, for there must have been in your life many similar ones. A smallish, not very important library meeting was dying on its feet, paralyzed with boredom and weariness. Then you came forward to read poetry to the group, as poetry ought to be read. You curtseyed for the dairy maid, you brought the fragrance of May and the sound of bells into that room . . . and life came back, and laughter, and imagination. I have never forgotten it.

This came from Elizabeth Coatsworth:

Whenever we go to Monhegan, coming out of the fog and the broad Atlantic, the focus of the village and of the scene is in a square grey house overlooking the harbor, which for more than a hundred years has been known as "The Influence." Something of its tranquility and strength is felt by every person on the island. There is no legend about it, no ghost, no remembered drama, but the quality of the house itself, and its curious name, make themselves felt in the life of the place, and set a standard without which the island would be much poorer. In every field of life, today as never before, our warm gratitude goes out to those who, like you, have been setters of standards, and guides in the vague harbors of the mind. For twentieth century children's literature you have been "The Influence," and a crowd of publishers and writers rise up to thank you for it.

Arthur B. Chrisman revealed that his Medal had been kept in a safety deposit box, "along with three shares of Montana copper stock and not much else," from the day he took it home. "Whenever I pay out two dollars and fifty cents a year just to keep a husky trinket secure from fire, theft, and the floods of Tick Creek, Arkansas, that shows I like it right well."

Said Eric Kelly: "The honor has always carried with it the obligation to produce nothing that may at a later time seem inferior to the book that won the award."

This scrapbook speaks eloquently for the Medals' early winners. The company thus assembled through their letters, for anniversary celebration in 1945, has expanded to include many more fellow winners, within the friendly bonds of Newbery-Caldecott. That they are writers and artists of good mettle, aware of their responsibility, is proven by the books that represent them. Persons with mean, ungenerous natures have nothing to say to children. Those with something worth saying, and a genuine talent for its expression, must possess certain virtues which become the human race: understanding and imagination, perhaps.

Their amiability and wholesome philosophy is shared in measure by the larger group concerned with children's books, the publishers, the critics, those who buy for personal use or for public shelves—because all these must live close to childhood's world. That world, holding its strong dominions in home, school, and library, developed its first art form in literature. From ageless fairy tales and nursery rhymes down to today's vibrant collections, the lineage is unbroken, and the character traits indestructible.

Librarians hold key influence over the uses of this literature. When Frederic Melcher chose them as custodians of the Newbery Medal he signified their unique interest, an interest which enables them to select and provide what is good as their most fundamental purpose. This is their single specialization. The whole history of these award Medals pays tribute to the taste and idealism of children's librarians in the Medals' first decades. These standards of selection to which the Medals testify may be reviewed by younger members at face value, for they came of staunch material.

The elders of children's librarianship, many of them named in this narrative, practiced one art exceedingly well. That art was, and is, knowledge of children's books, stored up year by year through constant, tireless, critical reading. For this knowledge there is no substitute; it is the essential absolute. It is solid bedrock in the stream of tradition which bears these Medals along through the seasons. The stream's source was Frederic Melcher; its sparkling current the creative winners of these honors he envisioned.

The Newbery and Caldecott Medals have realized their meaning in our day. We salute their donor, and the men for whom he named them. We applaud those who write and illustrate the worthy books, and the editors who, recognizing merit, give them form. Then finally, a cheer for the jury, the librarians through whose reading and reviewing, daily uses, and objective judgments the ultimate choice is made. Let all find welcome at the King's Breakfast.

# APPENDIX

# APPENDIX

## *1. Books That Have Won the Newbery Medal*

(The date in the left-hand column indicates the year in which the award was actually conferred. The date of publication follows the name of the original publisher. The name of the present publisher, if different from the original, is given in parentheses.)

1922   *The Story of Mankind* by Hendrik Willem Van Loon. Boni & Liveright, 1921. (Liveright)

1923   *The Voyages of Doctor Dolittle* by Hugh Lofting. Stokes, 1922. (Lippincott)

1924   *The Dark Frigate* by Charles Boardman Hawes. Little, Brown, 1923.

1925   *Tales from Silver Lands* by Charles J. Finger. Illustrated by Paul Honoré. Doubleday, Doran, 1924. (Doubleday)

1926   *Shen of the Sea* by Arthur Bowie Chrisman. Illustrated by Else Hasselriis. Dutton, 1925.

1927   *Smoky, the Cowhorse* by Will James. Scribner, 1926.

1928   *Gay Neck* by Dhan Gopal Mukerji. Illustrated by Boris Artzybasheff. Dutton, 1927.

1929   *Trumpeter of Krakow* by Eric P. Kelly. Illustrated by Angela Pruszynska. Macmillan, 1928.

1930   *Hitty, Her First Hundred Years* by Rachel Field. Illustrated by Dorothy P. Lathrop. Macmillan, 1929.

1931   *The Cat Who Went to Heaven* by Elizabeth Coatsworth. Illustrated by Lynd Ward. Macmillan, 1930.

1932    *Waterless Mountain* by Laura Adams Armer. Illustrated by Sidney Armer and the author. Longmans, Green, 1931. (McKay)

1933    *Young Fu of the Upper Yangtze* by Elizabeth Foreman Lewis. Illustrated by Kurt Wiese. Winston, 1932. (Holt, Rinehart and Winston)

1934    *Invincible Louisa* by Cornelia Meigs. Little, Brown, 1933.

1935    *Dobry* by Monica Shannon. Illustrated by Atanas Katchamakoff. Viking, 1934.

1936    *Caddie Woodlawn* by Carol Ryrie Brink. Illustrated by Kate Seredy. Macmillan, 1935.

1937    *Roller Skates* by Ruth Sawyer. Illustrated by Valenti Angelo. Viking, 1936.

1938    *The White Stag* by Kate Seredy. Viking, 1937.

1939    *Thimble Summer* by Elizabeth Enright. Farrar & Rinehart, 1938. (Holt, Rinehart and Winston)

1940    *Daniel Boone* by James H. Daugherty. Viking, 1939.

1941    *Call It Courage* by Armstrong Sperry. Macmillan, 1940.

1942    *The Matchlock Gun* by Walter D. Edmonds. Illustrated by Paul Lantz. Dodd, Mead, 1941.

1943    *Adam of the Road* by Elizabeth Janet Gray. Illustrated by Robert Lawson. Viking, 1942.

1944    *Johnny Tremain* by Esther Forbes. Illustrated by Lynd Ward. Houghton Mifflin, 1943.

1945    *Rabbit Hill* by Robert Lawson. Viking, 1944.

1946    *Strawberry Girl* by Lois Lenski. Lippincott, 1945.

1947    *Miss Hickory* by Carolyn Sherwin Bailey. Illustrated by Ruth Gannett. Viking, 1946.

1948    *The Twenty-One Balloons* by William Pène du Bois. Viking, 1947.

1949 *King of the Wind* by Marguerite Henry. Illustrated by Wesley Dennis. Rand McNally, 1948.

1950 *The Door in the Wall* by Marguerite deAngeli. Doubleday, 1949.

1951 *Amos Fortune, Free Man* by Elizabeth Yates. Illustrated by Nora Unwin. Aladdin, 1950. (Dutton)

1952 *Ginger Pye* by Eleanor Estes. Harcourt, Brace, 1951.

1953 *Secret of the Andes* by Ann Nolan Clark. Illustrated by Jean Charlot. Viking, 1952.

1954 *... And Now Miguel* by Joseph Krumgold. Illustrated by Jean Charlot. Crowell, 1953.

1955 *The Wheel on the School* by Meindert DeJong. Illustrated by Maurice Sendak. Harper, 1954.

1956 *"Carry On, Mr. Bowditch"* by Jean L. Latham. Houghton Mifflin, 1955.

1957 *Miracles on Maple Hill* by Virginia Sorensen. Illustrated by Beth and Joe Krush. Harcourt, Brace, 1956.

1958 *Rifles for Watie* by Harold Keith. Crowell, 1957.

1959 *The Witch of Blackbird Pond* by Elizabeth George Speare. Illustrated by W. T. Mars. Houghton Mifflin, 1958.

1960 *Onion John* by Joseph Krumgold. Illustrated by Symeon Shimin. Crowell, 1959.

1961 *Island of the Blue Dolphins* by Scott O'Dell. Houghton Mifflin, 1960.

1962 *The Bronze Bow* by Elizabeth George Speare. Houghton Mifflin, 1961.

1963 *A Wrinkle in Time* by Madeleine L'Engle. Farrar, Strauss, 1962.

## 2. Books That Have Won the Caldecott Medal

(The date in the left-hand column indicates the year in which the award was actually conferred. The date of publication follows the name of the original publisher. The name of the present publisher, if different from the original, is given in parentheses. When pictures and text are not by the same person, the author's name is in parentheses following the title.)

1938    *Animals of the Bible, a Picture Book* (text selected from the King James Bible by Helen Dean Fish), illustrated by Dorothy P. Lathrop. Stokes, 1937. (Lippincott)

1939    *Mei Li* by Thomas Handforth. Doubleday, 1938.

1940    *Abraham Lincoln* by Ingri and Edgar P. d'Aulaire. Doubleday, 1939.

1941    *They Were Strong and Good* by Robert Lawson. Viking, 1940.

1942    *Make Way for Ducklings* by Robert McCloskey. Viking, 1941.

1943    *The Little House* by Virginia Lee Burton. Houghton Mifflin, 1942.

1944    *Many Moons* (by James Thurber), illustrated by Louis Slobodkin. Harcourt, Brace, 1943.

1945    *Prayer for a Child* (by Rachel Field), pictures by Elizabeth Orton Jones. Macmillan, 1944.

1946    *The Rooster Crows* by Maud and Miska Petersham. Macmillan, 1945.

1947    *The Little Island* (by Golden MacDonald), illustrated by Leonard Weisgard. Doubleday, 1946.

1948    *White Snow, Bright Snow* (by Alvin Tresselt), illustrated by Roger Duvoisin. Lothrop, Lee & Shepard, 1947.

1949    *The Big Snow* by Berta and Elmer Hader. Macmillan, 1948.

1950    *Song of the Swallows* by Leo Politi. Scribner, 1949.

1951    *The Egg Tree* by Katharine Milhous. Scribner, 1950.

1952    *Finders Keepers* (by Will and Nicolas), illustrated by Nicolas Mordvinoff. Harcourt, Brace, 1951.

1953 *The Biggest Bear* by Lynd Ward. Houghton Mifflin, 1952.

1954 *Madeline's Rescue* by Ludwig Bemelmans. Viking, 1953.

1955 *Cinderella* (by Charles Perrault), illustrated by Marcia Brown. Scribner, 1954.

1956 *Frog Went a-Courtin'* (by John Langstaff), illustrated by Feodor Rojankovsky. Harcourt, Brace, 1955.

1957 *A Tree Is Nice* (by Janice May Udry), illustrated by Marc Simont. Harper, 1956.

1958 *Time of Wonder* by Robert McCloskey. Viking, 1957.

1959 *Chanticleer and the Fox* by Barbara Cooney. Crowell, 1958.

1960 *Nine Days to Christmas* (by Marie Hall Ets and Aurora Labastida), illustrated by Marie Hall Ets. Viking, 1959.

1961 *Baboushka and the Three Kings* (by Ruth Robbins), illustrated by Nicolas Sidjakov. Parnassus, 1960.

1962 *Once A Mouse . . .* by Marcia Brown. Scribner, 1961.

1963 *The Snowy Day* by Ezra Jack Keats. Viking, 1962.

## 3. Runners-Up for the Newbery Medal

(The date in the left-hand column indicates the year of publication. Out-of-print books are marked o.p.)

1921 *The Great Quest,* by Charles Boardman Hawes, Little, Brown. (o.p.)
*Cedric the Forester,* by Bernard G. Marshall, Appleton-Century. (o.p.)
*The Old Tobacco Shop,* by William Bowen, Macmillan. (o.p.)
*The Golden Fleece,* by Padraic Colum, Macmillan.
*Windy Hill,* by Cornelia Meigs, Macmillan. (o.p.)

1922    no record

1923    no record

1924    *Nicholas,* by Anne Carroll Moore, Putnam. (o.p.)
*Dream Coach,* by Anne and Dillwyn Parrish, Macmillan. (o.p.)

1925    *The Voyagers,* by Padraic Colum, Macmillan. (o.p.)

1926    no record

1927    *The Wonder-Smith and His Son,* by Ella Young, Longmans, Green. (McKay)
*Downright Dencey,* by Caroline Dale Snedeker, Doubleday, Doran. (Doubleday)

1928    *The Pigtail of Ah Lee Ben Loo,* by John Bennett, Longmans, Green. (o.p.)
*Millions of Cats,* by Wanda Gág, Coward-McCann.
*The Boy Who Was,* by Grace T. Hallock, Dutton. (o.p.)
*Clearing Weather,* by Cornelia Meigs, Little, Brown. (o.p.)
*The Runaway Papoose,* by Grace P. Moon, Doubleday, Doran. (o.p.)
*Tod of the Fens,* by Eleanor Whitney, Macmillan. (o.p.)

1929    *Pran of Albania,* by Elizabeth C. Miller, Doubleday, Doran. (o.p.)
*The Jumping-Off Place,* by Marian Hurd McNeely, Longmans, Green. (McKay)
*A Daughter of the Seine,* by Jeanette Eaton, Harper. (o.p.)

1930    *Floating Island,* by Anne Parrish, Harper.
*The Dark Star of Itza,* by Alida Malkus, Harcourt, Brace. (o.p.)
*Queer Person,* by Ralph Hubbard, Doubleday, Doran. (o.p.)
*Mountains Are Free,* by Julia Davis Adams, Dutton. (o.p.)

1930 *Spice and the Devil's Cave,* by Agnes D. Hewes, Knopf.

*Meggy MacIntosh,* by Elizabeth Janet Gray, Doubleday, Doran. (Viking)

1931 *The Fairy Circus,* by Dorothy Lathrop, Macmillan. (o.p.)

*Calico Bush,* by Rachel Field, Macmillan.

*Boy of the South Seas,* by Eunice Tietjens, Coward-McCann. (o.p.)

*Out of the Flame,* by Eloise Lounsbery, Longmans, Green. (o.p.)

*Jane's Island,* by Marjorie Hill Allee, Houghton Mifflin. (o.p.)

*Truce of the Wolf,* by Mary Gould Davis, Harcourt, Brace. (o.p.)

1932 *Hepatica Hawks,* by Rachel Field, Macmillan.

*Romantic Rebel,* by Hildegarde Hawthorne, Appleton-Century. (Meredith)

*Auntie,* by Maud and Miska Petersham, Doubleday, Doran. (o.p.)

*Tirra Lirra,* by Laura E. Richards, Little, Brown.

*Little House in the Big Woods,* by Laura Ingalls Wilder, Harper.

1933 *Forgotten Daughter,* by Caroline Dale Snedeker, Doubleday, Doran.

*Swords of Steel,* by Elsie Singmaster, Houghton Mifflin. (o.p.)

*ABC Bunny,* by Wanda Gág, Coward-McCann.

*Winged Girl of Knossos,* by Erick Berry, Appleton-Century. (o.p.)

*New Land,* by Sarah L. Schmidt, McBride. (o.p.)

*Apprentice of Florence,* by Anne Kyle, Houghton Mifflin. (o.p.)

1934 *The Pageant of Chinese History,* by Elizabeth Seeger, Longmans, Green. (McKay)

1934    *Davy Crockett,* by Constance Rourke, Harcourt, Brace.

*A Day on Skates,* by Hilda Van Stockum, Harper. (o.p.)

1935    *Honk the Moose,* by Phil Stong, Dodd, Mead.
*The Good Master,* by Kate Seredy, Viking.
*Young Walter Scott,* by Elizabeth Janet Gray, Viking.
*All Sail Set,* by Armstrong Sperry, Winston. (o.p.)

1936    *Phebe Fairchild: Her Book,* by Lois Lenski, Stokes. (Lippincott)
*Whistler's Van,* by Idwal Jones, Viking. (o.p.)
*The Golden Basket,* by Ludwig Bemelmans, Viking. (o.p.)
*Winterbound,* by Margery Bianco, Viking.
*Audubon,* by Constance Rourke, Harcourt, Brace. (o.p.)
*The Codfish Musket,* by Agnes D. Hewes, Doubleday, Doran. (o.p.)

1937    *Bright Island,* by Mabel L. Robinson, Random House.
*Pecos Bill,* by James Cloyd Bowman, Whitman.
*On the Banks of Plum Creek,* by Laura Ingalls Wilder, Harper.

1938    *Leader by Destiny,* by Jeanette Eaton, Harcourt, Brace.
*Penn,* by Elizabeth Janet Gray, Viking.
*Nino,* by Valenti Angelo, Viking.
*"Hello, the Boat!"* by Phyllis Crawford, Holt. (Holt, Rinehart and Winston)
*Mr. Popper's Penguins,* by Richard and Florence Atwater, Little, Brown.

1939    *The Singing Tree,* by Kate Seredy, Viking.
*Runner of the Mountain Tops,* by Mabel L. Robinson, Random House. (o.p.)
*By the Shores of Silver Lake,* by Laura Ingalls Wilder, Harper.

1939 *Boy with a Pack,* by Stephen W. Meader, Harcourt, Brace.

1940 *Blue Willow,* by Doris Gates, Viking.
*Young Mac of Fort Vancouver,* by Mary Jane Carr, Crowell.
*The Long Winter,* by Laura Ingalls Wilder, Harper.
*Nansen,* by Anna Gertrude Hall, Viking.

1941 *Little Town on the Prairie,* by Laura Ingalls Wilder, Harper.
*George Washington's World,* by Genevieve Foster, Scribner.
*Indian Captive,* by Lois Lenski, Stokes. (Lippincott)
*Down Ryton Water,* by E. R. Gaggin, Viking. (o.p.)

1942 *The Middle Moffat,* by Eleanor Estes, Harcourt, Brace.
*"Have You Seen Tom Thumb?"* by Mabel Leigh Hunt, Stokes. (Lippincott)

1943 *These Happy Golden Years,* by Laura Ingalls Wilder, Harper.
*Fog Magic,* by Julia L. Sauer, Viking.
*Rufus M.,* by Eleanor Estes, Harcourt, Brace.
*Mountain Born,* by Elizabeth Yates, Coward-McCann.

1944 *The Hundred Dresses,* by Eleanor Estes, Harcourt, Brace.
*The Silver Pencil,* by Alice Dalgliesh, Scribner.
*Abraham Lincoln's World,* by Genevieve Foster, Scribner.
*Lone Journey,* by Jeannette Eaton, Harcourt, Brace.

1945 *Justin Morgan Had a Horse,* by Marguerite Henry, Wilcox & Follett. (Rand McNally)
*The Moved-Outers,* by Florence Crannell Means, Houghton Mifflin.
*Bhimsa, the Dancing Bear,* by Christine Weston, Scribner. (o.p.)

1945    *New Found World,* by Katherine B. Shippen, Viking.

1946    *The Wonderful Year,* by Nancy Barnes, Messner.
*Big Tree,* by Mary and Conrad Buff, Viking.
*The Heavenly Tenants,* by William Maxwell, Harper.
(o.p.)
*The Avion My Uncle Flew,* by Cyrus Fisher, Appleton-Century. (Meredith)
*The Hidden Treasure of Glaston,* by Eleanore M. Jewett, Viking.

1947    *Pancakes-Paris,* by Claire Huchet Bishop, Viking.
*Li Lun, Lad of Courage,* by Carolyn Treffinger, Abingdon-Cokesbury. (Abingdon)
*The Quaint and Curious Quest of Johnny Longfoot,* by Catherine Besterman, Bobbs-Merrill. (o.p.)
*The Cow-Tail Switch,* by Harold Courlander and George Herzog, Holt.
*Misty of Chincoteague,* by Marguerite Henry, Rand McNally.

1948    *Seabird,* by Holling Clancy Holling, Houghton Mifflin.
*Daughter of the Mountains,* by Louise Rankin, Viking.
*My Father's Dragon,* by Ruth S. Gannett, Random House.
*Story of the Negro,* by Arna Bontemps, Knopf.

1949    *Tree of Freedom,* by Rebecca Caudill, Viking.
*Blue Cat of Castle Town,* by Catherine Coblentz, Longmans, Green. (McKay)
*Kildee House,* by Rutherford Montgomery, Doubleday.
*George Washington,* by Genevieve Foster, Scribner.
*Song of the Pines,* by Walter and Marion Havighurst, Winston.

1950    *Better Known as Johnny Appleseed,* by Mabel Leigh Hunt, Lippincott.

1950    *Gandhi, Fighter without a Sword,* by Jeanette Eaton, Morrow.
*Abraham Lincoln, Friend of the People,* by Clara I. Judson, Wilcox & Follett. (Follett)
*The Story of Appleby Capple,* by Anne Parrish, Harper. (o.p.)

1951    *Americans Before Columbus,* by Elizabeth Chesley Baity, Viking.
*Minn of the Mississippi,* by Holling Clancy Holling, Houghton Mifflin.
*The Defender,* by Nicholas Kalashnikoff, Scribner.
*The Light at Tern Rock,* by Julia L. Sauer, Viking.
*The Apple and the Arrow,* by Mary and Conrad Buff, Houghton Mifflin.

1952    *Charlotte's Web,* by E. B. White, Harper.
*Moccasin Trail,* by Eloise J. McGraw, Coward-McCann.
*Red Sails to Capri,* by Ann Weil, Viking.
*The Bears on Hemlock Mountain,* by Alice Dalgliesh, Scribner.
*Birthdays of Freedom,* by Genevieve Foster, Scribner.

1953    *All Alone,* by Claire Huchet Bishop, Viking.
*Shadrach,* by Meindert DeJong, Harper.
*Hurry Home, Candy,* by Meindert DeJong, Harper.
*Theodore Roosevelt, Fighting Patriot,* by Clara I. Judson, Follett.
*Magic Maize,* by Mary and Conrad Buff, Houghton, Mifflin.

1954    *The Courage of Sarah Noble,* by Alice Dalgliesh, Scribner.
*Banner in the Sky,* by James Ramsay Ullman, Lippincott.

1955    *The Golden Name Day,* by Jennie D. Lindquist, Harper.

1955    *The Secret River,* by Marjorie Kinnan Rawlings, Scribner.
*Men, Microscopes, and Living Things,* by Katherine B. Shippen, Viking.

1956    *Old Yeller,* by Fred Gipson, Harper.
*The House of Sixty Fathers,* by Meindert DeJong, Harper.
*Mr. Justice Holmes,* by Clara I. Judson, Follett.
*The Corn Grows Ripe,* by Dorothy Rhoads, Viking.
*Black Fox of Lorne,* by Marguerite deAngeli, Doubleday.

1957    *The Horsecatcher,* by Mari Sandoz, Westminster.
*Gone-Away Lake,* by Elizabeth Enright, Harcourt, Brace.
*The Great Wheel,* by Robert Lawson, Viking.
*Tom Paine, Freedom's Apostle,* by Leo Gurko, Crowell.

1958    *The Family Under the Bridge,* by Natalie Savage Carlson, Harper.
*Along Came a Dog,* by Meindert DeJong, Harper.
*Chúcaro, Wild Pony of the Pampa,* by Francis Kalnay, Harcourt, Brace.
*The Perilous Road,* by William O. Steele, Harcourt, Brace.

1959    *My Side of the Mountain,* by Jean George, Dutton.
*America Is Born,* by Gerald Johnson, Morrow.
*The Gammage Cup,* by Carol Kendall, Harcourt, Brace.

1960    *America Moves Forward,* by Gerald Johnson, Morrow.
*Old Ramon,* by Jack Schaefer, Houghton Mifflin.
*The Cricket in Times Square,* by George Selden, Farrar, Strauss.

1961    *Frontier Living,* by Edwin Tunis, World.

1961 *The Golden Goblet,* by Eloise McGraw, Coward-McCann.
*Belling the Tiger,* by Mary Stolz, Harper.

1962 *Thistle and Thyme,* by Sorche Nic Leodhas, Holt, Rinehart and Winston.
*Men of Athens,* by Olivia Coolidge, Houghton Mifflin.

## 4. Runners-Up for the Caldecott Medal

(The date in the left-hand column indicates the year of publication. When pictures and text are not by the same person, the author's name is in parentheses.)

1937 *Seven Simeons,* by Boris Artzybasheff, Viking.
*Four and Twenty Blackbirds* (compiled by Helen Dean Fish), illustrated by Robert Lawson, Stokes. (Lippincott)

1938 *The Forest Pool,* by Laura Adams Armer, Longmans, Green. (o.p.)
*Wee Gillis* (by Munro Leaf), illustrated by Robert Lawson, Viking.
*Snow White and the Seven Dwarfs,* translated and illustrated by Wanda Gág, Coward-McCann.

1938 *Barkis,* by Clare Turlay Newberry, Harper.
*Andy and the Lion,* by James Daugherty, Viking.

1939 *Cock-a-Doodle-Doo,* by Berta and Elmer Hader, Macmillan. (Viking)
*Madeline,* by Ludwig Bemelmans, Simon & Schuster.
*The Ageless Story,* by Lauren Ford, Dodd, Mead. (o.p.)

1940 *April's Kittens,* by Clare Turlay Newberry, Harper.

1941 *An American ABC,* by Maud and Miska Petersham, Macmillan.
*In My Mother's House* (by Ann Nolan Clark), illustrated by Velino Herrera, Viking.

1941    *Paddle-to-the-Sea,* by Holling Clancy Holling, Houghton Mifflin.
*Nothing at All,* by Wanda Gág, Coward-McCann.

1942    *Dash and Dart,* by Mary and Conrad Buff, Viking.
*Marshmallow,* by Clare Turlay Newberry, Harper.

1943    *Small Rain* (text arranged from the Bible by Jessie Orton Jones), illustrated by Elizabeth Orton Jones, Viking.
*Pierre Pidgeon* (by Lee Kingman), illustrated by Arnold Edwin Bare, Houghton Mifflin. (o.p.)
*Good-Luck Horse* (by Chih-Yi Chan), illustrated by Plato Chan, Whittlesey. (o.p.)
*Mighty Hunter,* by Berta and Elmer Hader, Macmillan.
*A Child's Good Night Book* (by Margaret Wise Brown), illustrated by Jean Charlot, William R. Scott.

1944    *Mother Goose,* compiled and illustrated by Tasha Tudor, Oxford. (Walck)
*In the Forest,* by Marie Hall Ets, Viking.
*Yonie Wondernose,* by Marguerite deAngeli, Doubleday.
*The Christmas Anna Angel* (by Ruth Sawyer), illustrated by Kate Seredy, Viking.

1945    *Little Lost Lamb* (by Margaret Wise Brown), illustrated by Leonard Weisgard, Doubleday.
*Sing Mother Goose* (music by Opal Wheeler), illustrated by Marjorie Torrey, Dutton.
*My Mother Is the Most Beautiful Woman in the World* (by Rebecca Reyher), illustrated by Ruth C. Gannett, Lothrop.
*You Can Write Chinese,* by Kurt Wiese, Viking.

1946    *Rain Drop Splash* (by Alvin R. Tresselt), illustrated by Leonard Weisgard, Lothrop.
*Boats on the River* (by Marjorie Flack), illustrated by Jay Hyde Barnum, Viking.

1946   *Timothy Turtle* (by Al Graham), illustrated by Tony Palazzo, Robert Welch. (Viking)
   *Pedro, the Angel of Olvera Street,* by Leo Politi, Scribner.
   *Sing in Praise* (by Opal Wheeler), illustrated by Marjorie Torrey, Dutton.

1947   *Stone Soup,* told and illustrated by Marcia Brown, Scribner.
   *McEligot's Pool,* by Theodor S. Geisel [Dr. Seuss], Random House.
   *Bambino the Clown,* by George Schreiber, Viking.
   *Roger and the Fox* (by Lavinia R. Davis), illustrated by Hildegard Woodward, Doubleday.
   *Song of Robin Hood* (edited by Anne Malcolmson), illustrated by Virginia Lee Burton, Houghton Mifflin.

1948   *Blueberries for Sal,* by Robert McCloskey, Viking.
   *All Around the Town* (by Phyllis McGinley), illustrated by Helen Stone, Lippincott.
   *Juanita,* by Leo Politi, Scribner.
   *Fish in the Air,* by Kurt Wiese, Viking.

1949   *America's Ethan Allen* (by Stewart Holbrook), illustrated by Lynd Ward, Houghton Mifflin.
   *The Wild Birthday Cake* (by Lavinia R. Davis), illustrated by Hildegard Woodward, Doubleday.
   *Happy Day* (by Ruth Krauss), illustrated by Marc Simont, Harper.
   *Henry—Fisherman,* by Marcia Brown, Scribner.
   *Bartholomew and the Oobleck,* by Theodor S. Geisel [Dr. Seuss], Random House.

1950   *Dick Whittington and His Cat,* told and illustrated by Marcia Brown, Scribner.
   *The Two Reds* (by William [Lipkind]), illustrated by Nicolas [Mordvinoff], Harcourt, Brace.
   *If I Ran the Zoo,* by Theodor Geisel [Dr. Seuss], Random House.

1950    *T-Bone the Baby-Sitter,* by Clare Turlay Newberry, Harper.

*The Most Wonderful Doll in the World* (by Phyllis McGinley), illustrated by Helen Stone, Lippincott.

1951    *Mr. T. W. Anthony Woo,* by Marie Hall Ets, Viking.

*Skipper John's Cook,* by Marcia Brown, Scribner.

*All Falling Down* (by Gene Zion), illustrated by Margaret B. Graham, Harper.

*Bear Party,* by William Pène du Bois, Viking.

*Feather Mountain,* by Elizabeth Olds, Houghton Mifflin.

1952    *Puss in Boots,* told and illustrated by Marcia Brown, Scribner.

*One Morning in Maine,* by Robert McCloskey, Viking.

*Ape in a Cape,* by Fritz Eichenberg, Harcourt, Brace.

*The Storm Book* (by Charlotte Zolotow), illustrated by Margaret B. Graham, Harper.

*Five Little Monkeys,* by Juliet Kepes, Houghton Mifflin.

1953    *Journey Cake, Ho!* (by Ruth Sawyer), illustrated by Robert McCloskey, Viking.

*When Will the World Be Mine?* (by Miriam Schlein), illustrated by Jean Charlot, William R. Scott. (o.p.)

*The Steadfast Tin Soldier* (translated by M. R. James), adapted from Hans Christian Andersen and illustrated by Marcia Brown, Scribner.

*A Very Special House* (by Ruth Krauss), illustrated by Maurice Sendak, Harper.

*Green Eyes,* by Abe Birnbaum, Capitol. (Golden)

1954    *Book of Nursery and Mother Goose Rhymes,* compiled and illustrated by Marguerite deAngeli, Doubleday.

*Wheel on the Chimney* (by Margaret Wise Brown), illustrated by Tibor Gergely, Lippincott.

1955    *Play with Me,* by Marie Hall Ets, Viking.

1955    *Crow Boy,* by Taro Yashima, Viking.

1956    *Mr. Penny's Race Horse,* by Marie Hall Ets, Viking.
        *1 Is One,* by Tasha Tudor, Oxford. (Walck)
        *Anatole* (by Eve Titus), illustrated by Paul Galdone,
        Whittlesey.
        *Gillespie and the Guards* (by Benjamin Elkin), illus-
        trated by James Daugherty, Viking.
        *Lion,* by William Pène du Bois, Viking.

1957    *Fly High, Fly Low,* by Don Freeman, Viking.
        *Anatole and the Cat* (by Eve Titus), illustrated by
        Paul Galdone, Whittlesey.

1958    *The House That Jack Built,* by Antonio Frasconi,
        Harcourt, Brace.
        *What Do You Say, Dear?* (by Seslye Joslin), illus-
        trated by Maurice Sendak, William R. Scott.
        *Umbrella,* by Taro Yashima, Viking.

1959    *Houses from the Sea* (by Alice Goudey), illustrated
        by Adrienne Adams, Scribner.
        *Moon Jumpers,* by Maurice Sendak, Harper.

1960    *Inch by Inch,* by Leo Leonni, Obolensky.

1961    *The Fox Went Out on a Chilly Night,* by Peter Spier,
        Doubleday.
        *Little Bear's Visit* (by Else Holmeland Minarik), il-
        lustrated by Maurice Sendak, Harper.
        *The Day We Saw the Sun Come Up* (by Alice
        Goudey), illustrated by Adrienne Adams, Scribner.

1962    *The Sun Is a Golden Earring,* by Bernarda Bryson,
        Holt, Rinehart and Winston.
        *Mr. Rabbit and the Lovely Present* (by Charlotte
        Zolotow), illustrated by Maurice Sendak, Harper.

# INDEX

# INDEX